VERY

102 Teachable Films

JOSEPH KENNEDY • ELIZABETH MEJIA • MAIDA KENNEDY XIAO

PRENTICE HALL REGENTS
ENGLEWOOD CLIFFS, NEW JERSEY

Library of Congress Cataloging-in-Publication Data

Mejia, Elizabeth A., 1958–
    102 very teachable films / Elizabeth Mejia, Maida Kennedy Xiao,
Joseph Kennedy
        p.   cm.
        Includes bibliographical references and indexes.
        ISBN 0–13–106824–5: $15.95
        1. English language—Study and teaching—Foreign speakers—Audio-visual aids—Catalogs.
2. English language—Films for foreign speakers—Catalogs.   I. Kennedy Xiao, Maida, 1961–   .
II. Kennedy, Joseph, 1959–   .   III. Title.   IV. Title: One hundred two very teachable films.
Z5818.E5M45   1994
[PE1128.A2]
016.428'0078—dc20   94–17393 CIP

Acquisitions Editor: Nancy Baxer
Director of Production and Manufacturing: David Riccardi
Editorial Production / Design Manager: Dominick Mosco
Electronic Production Coordinator: Molly Pike Riccardi
Electronic production and interior page design: D. Andrew Gitzy
Cover Design Coordinator: Merle Krumper
Production Coordinators: Ray Keating and David Dickey

© 1994 by PRENTICE HALL REGENTS
Prentice-Hall, Inc.
A Paramount Communications Company
Englewood Cliffs, New Jersey 07632

Printed in the United States of America

10   9   8   7   6   5   4   3   2   1

ISBN 0-13-106824-5

Prentice Hall International (UK) Limited, London
Prentice Hall of Australia Pty. Limited, Sydney
Prentice Hall Canada, Inc., Toronto
Prentice Hall Hispanoamericana, S.A., Mexico
Prentice Hall Of India Private Limited, New Delhi
Prentice Hall of Japan, Inc., Tokyo
Simon & Schuster Asia Pte. Ltd., Singapore
Editora Prentice Hall do Brasil, Ltda., Rio de Janeiro

ACKNOWLEDGMENTS

The authors would like to express their deepest appreciation to Mathilde Kennedy, their mother, who provided all the authors with invaluable assistance in writing this book and without whose help this book would not have been completed.

Joseph Kennedy, Maida Kennedy Xiao, Elizabeth Mejia

For my daughter Pamela, my ongoing reason to keep going on.

Elizabeth Mejia

For my children, Justin, Mei Mei, and Pei Pei, who were so patient and loving while I worked on this project.

Maida Kennedy Xiao

For my wife, Tina.

Joseph Kennedy

HOW TO USE THIS BOOK

"A Picture Is Worth a Thousand Words"

Movies are a very useful resource for teaching a subject, yet the need for visual schema is often overlooked in classrooms. Teachers routinely teach historical and cultural periods, such as the Roaring Twenties, without ever giving their students a sense of what the period looked like. Movies can make a subject such as China's Forbidden City more real if students can see how it actually looks. For ESL students, movies can provide cultural insight that would otherwise be hard to gain. In addition, since movies are a popular art and entertainment form, they are usually well received by students. Finally, the use of movies in the classroom helps students develop critical-viewing skills through the analysis and follow-up activities.

What This Book Is and Is Not

This book is a reference guide to movies that teachers can use in classes from the junior high through community college levels, as well as in classes of ESL students from intermediate through advanced levels. It is designed to help the teacher choose the appropriate movie and to provide him or her with ideas for using the movie.

This book is not a substitute for watching the movies. It is merely a guide that can be used in selecting a film to preview before showing it to a class. Each teacher needs to select movies by taking into account such factors as school policies, appropriateness of subject matter, and level of difficulty of language. The authors do not accept responsibility for problems arising from a teacher's selection of a movie for a particular class.

Components of the Book

There are two ways to locate a movie in this book. If you know the name of the movie, you can use the Title Index. If, however, you know only the subject of the movie you need, use the Subject Index to locate the movie. In addition, the first line of each entry lists subjects, by number, that are keyed to the Subject Index. Looking in the Subject Index under those numbers will provide listings of other films in the same categories.

Each entry includes the following parts.

- A *Plot Summary* tells enough of the plot to provide an idea of what the movie is about.

- A *General Commentary* reviews the strengths and weaknesses of the movie, including its appropriateness for various audiences.

- A *List of Suggested Usage* is divided into previewing, viewing, and follow-up activities. These lists are neither definitive nor exhaustive and are designed to spark ideas for ways a movie can be used in a class.

- A *List of Other Considerations* notes points of the movie that might pose difficulty for some teachers in some situations. There aren't many of these because this book contains *102 Very Teachable Films!*

- A *List of Ancillary Materials* can be used by teachers to acquire background information about the topics covered in a film. These materials are not necessarily appropriate for students.

Vocabulary You Will See in the Suggested Usage Lists

1. Research

   Many of the activities we suggest involve research. In some cases, we make specific suggestions about research materials that can be used, although in most cases encyclopedias will be sufficient. Simple research ideas include having the students read material on the same topic from different encyclopedias and then synthesize what they have learned in small groups before writing up their results.

2. Report

   You may wish to have students report on their research orally or in writing. Students should be encouraged to use their own words and to keep their reports focused on the important information.

3. Compare

   In many places we suggest that students be asked to compare literature with film or film with film.

4. Scenes Critical for Comprehension

   When we use this phrase we refer to scenes that are absolutely essential to understanding the story. Most movies have at least one such scene; some have more. In any case, these scenes are ideal places to do comprehension checks.

5. Comprehension Checks

   Comprehension checks are oral questions after a scene to determine that students understand the scene. A simple methodology for a comprehension check is to stop the tape immediately after the critical scene and ask three to five basic questions about the scene. Then play the scene again to ensure that all students have a chance to fix it in their minds.

6. Reported / Mute / Paired Narrations

   This series of terms comes from ESL methodology. The terms are designed to promote discussion and comprehension. In a mute narration, two partners look at a scene with the sound off and discuss what they think is being discussed in the scene. This approach is particularly useful with scenes in which body language, facial expressions, and/or actions are helpful in supporting comprehension. In a paired narration, one student watches the scene and tells another, who cannot see the screen, what is happening. This technique helps students to use present tenses and to describe. A reported narration is like a paired narration except that the reporter describes the scene to another student after it is over, which requires the use of the past tense. For more on these methodologies, teachers are advised to refer to *Five Star Films* by Mejia and O'Connor.

We hope you find this book useful, and we welcome your comments.

The Adventures of Huck Finn

Subjects:	1, 10, 13, 16, 17, 23	**Director:**	Stephen Sommers
Playing Time:	108 minutes	**Producer:**	Laurence Mark
Rating:	PG	**Date:**	1993
		Actors:	Elijah Wood, Courtney B. Vance, Ron Perlman, Jason Robards

Plot Summary

This movie sticks closely to the plot developed in the book by Mark Twain. Huck Finn, accompanied by an escaped slave, is fleeing from an abusive father and a confining life. Down the Mississippi they go, and this film relates their adventures as they meet flimflam men, feuding families, and a host of other incredible characters. The journey serves as a vehicle for Huck's coming of age as he learns that just because society says something is right (like slavery) doesn't make it right. All the wiser for this wisdom, the travelers end up in St. Petersburg, their original point of departure, where Jim, the runaway slave, finds he's a free man and Huck is left counting his blessings that he's alive.

General Commentary

Two points make this film special: the extraordinary talents of the supporting cast of characters, and the absolute brutality with which Huck's family life is portrayed. The movie shows the similarity between Huck and many modern, abused children left to fend for themselves and grow up on their own. This theme is sometimes explored in interpretations of *Huck Finn*, but in this version the point is made painfully clear. One realizes that, although *Huck Finn* was set in an era more than a century ago, it is still a thoroughly modern story. The film is excellent for students from junior high school through college and in ESL classes.

Suggested Usage

Previewing Activities

- Students can read the story by Mark Twain. ESL teachers may wish to consider a relatively dialect-free write-down, such as the excellent Longman Simplified English edition.

- Depending on resources available, students can read about and research runaway slave laws and famous runaway slaves in literature. Selected passages from *Roots*, *Uncle Tom's Cabin*, and *Scenes in the Life of Harriet Tubman* are excellent vehicles for generating discussion of the penalties slaves faced for running away.

Viewing Activities

GOOD PLACES TO STOP AND TALK

- ESL students may find it beneficial to stop for comprehension checks after the following scenes:

  the scene in which Huck is stolen by his father

  the scene in which Huck finds Jim hiding out on the island

  the scene in which Huck and Jim end up on the plantation of the feuding family

  the scene in which Huck and Jim hook up with the con men

- The following scenes can be used for reported / paired / mute viewing by ESL students:

  the scene in which Huck escapes from his home

  the scene in which Huck meets Jim

  the scene in which Huck hides the money in the coffin

  the scene in which Jim is almost hung

PATTERNS/STRUCTURES TO LOOK FOR

- For follow-up discussion, students can be asked to track different streams in this story. The two most obvious are *Huck Finn* as the story of an abused child, and *Huck Finn* as an anti-slavery story. Students can be divided into two groups, with one group looking for evidence of former and the other looking for evidence of the latter.

Follow-up Activities

- Students can compare the novel with the movie.
- Students can present a defense of one of the following two opinions: (a) *Huck Finn* is basically the story of an abused child learning what the world is about; or (b) *Huck Finn* is basically a story that attacks the institution of slavery.
- Students can research some of the more current evidence that suggests that Twain modeled Huck Finn on a black child, and can report on that evidence.
- Students can compare the life of Huck Finn to an account of an abused child.

Other Considerations

A few scenes of graphic child abuse might be particularly disturbing to younger students.

Ancillary Material

Twain, Mark. *The Adventures of Huckleberry Finn.* Berkeley: University of California Press, 1985.

Twain, Mark. *The Adventures of Huckleberry Finn.* Longman Simplified English Series.

Bradford, Sarah H. *Scenes in the Life of Harriet Tubman.* Auburn, N.Y.: W.J. Moses, 1869.

Haley, Alex. *Roots.* Garden City, N.Y.: Doubleday, 1976.

Stowe, Harriet Beecher. *Uncle Tom's Cabin and A Key to Uncle Tom's Cabin.* Hildesheim, N.Y.: G. Oms Verlag, 1975.

The African Queen

Subjects: 1, 14, 25, 30
Playing Time: 105 minutes
Rating: not rated

Director: John Huston
Producer: Sam Spiegel
Date: 1951
Actors: Humphrey Bogart, Robert Morley, Katharine Hepburn, Theodore Bikel

Plot Summary

In East Africa at the beginning of World War I, Charlie Allnut uses his little steamer, *The African Queen*, to run supplies for small villages. At one village he meets Rose Sayer, the sister of missionary Reverend Samuel Sayer. While Charlie continues his supply run, the Germans invade the village and kill Rev. Sayer. When Charlie returns he finds Rose mourning the loss of her brother. Charlie takes Rose out of the jungle on his boat. The river ride is dangerous and exciting and brings these two opposites together. Eventually they reach their destination and do their part in the war against the Germans.

General Commentary

This war, romance, and adventure is a classic! From the on-location filming in Africa to the witty dialogue, nothing is missing. This film can be used in any class studying world history and imperialism. Everyone should see this film if for no other reason than to view the film that gave Bogart his only Oscar.

Suggested Usage

Previewing Activities

- Students can research the expansion of the German Empire before World War I.
- Students can examine maps of Africa from 1900 to 1920 to find how Africa changed during that period of time.

Viewing Activities

GOOD PLACES TO STOP AND TALK

- Teachers might want to stop and have students predict what will happen on Charlie and Rose's journey down the river. Students can write down their predictions for use at a later time.

PATTERNS/STRUCTURES TO LOOK FOR

- It is useful for ESL students to listen for any scene in which Rose and Charlie are involved in "combative dialogue" and to note the way in which the two disagree. This could involve looking for body language as well as listening for verbal discourse.

Follow-up Activities

- Students can now work with their earlier predictions. How did their predictions differ from what really happened? Were there any clues that helped in the predictions?
- Students can research German aggression in Africa during World War II to answer the following type of question: How did German geographic conquests differ in each World War?
- History teachers may want to have students check the accuracy of the film in regards to German imperialism in Africa.

Other Considerations

None.

Ancillary Material

Bridgman, John. *German Africa: A Select Annotated Bibliography.* Palo Alto, Calif.: Stanford University, Hoover Institution on War, Revolution, and Peace, 1965.

Air America

Subjects:	1, 9, 22, 28	**Director:**	Roger Spottiswoode
Playing Time:	112 minutes	**Producer:**	Daniel Melnick
Rating:	R	**Date:**	1990
		Actors:	Mel Gibson, Robert Downey Jr.

Plot Summary

This story about American pilots flying for the CIA in Laos during the Vietnam War centers around two pilots. Gene is a veteran pilot who has a Laotian wife and runs guns when he is not flying CIA-sponsored planes that drop pigs and rice from the sky. Billy is a young recruit from southern California. The story is mostly about the U.S. government's hypocritical relationships with Southeast Asian leaders and the U.S. government's attempt to cover up its activities in Laos.

General Commentary

There are holes in this movie's plot. For example, Gene's superficial relationship with his wife is never explored in any detail. Many of the characters (such as the American and Laotian military officials, the U.S. senator, and the U.S. social worker) are more like caricatures than real people. However, the film does raise some good questions about America's involvement in Southeast Asia and is recommended for all types of classes.

Suggested Usage

Previewing Activities

- Students can locate Laos on a map.
- Students can research America's involvement in Laos and what happened in Laos.

Viewing Activities

GOOD PLACES TO STOP AND TALK

- An ESL teacher might do comprehension checks on the first two scenes, which introduce the two main characters and the background of the movie.
- ESL students can view the scene in the restaurant where the retired American military official, his young assistant, Rob, and the senator are speaking. Rob's facial expressions reveal his confusion at what is being said. Students can view the scene carefully to see how Rob expresses his confusion nonverbally.

PATTERNS/STRUCTURES TO LOOK FOR

- A number of scenes in this movie use sarcasm. ESL teachers can use these as teaching opportunities. For example, in the scene in the bar where Gene realizes that Billy is going to bomb the drug lab, he says that sounds like "unplanned fun." The same scene is also good for teaching students how to listen for implication.

Follow-up Activities

- Students can research the most famous CIA-sponsored air service, The Flying Tigers.
- Students can research and report on other CIA-sponsored covert activities. For this purpose, the film *Missing* is a useful follow-up.

Other Considerations

Teachers probably should not use this film by itself to teach about American involvement in Southeast Asia since it merely touches on many of the important issues of this topic.

Ancillary Material

Schultz, Duane P. *The Maverick War: Chennault and the Flying Tigers.* New York: St. Martin's Press, 1987.

All Quiet on the Western Front

Subjects:	10, 14, 17, 19, 30	**Director:**	Lewis Milestone
Playing Time:	140 minutes	**Producer:**	Carl Laemmie
	(black & white)	**Date:**	1930
Rating:	PG	**Actors:**	Louis Wolhiem, Lew Ayers, John Wray

Plot Summary

This movie is about war, youth, and how to survive the horrors of the battlefield. The story is set during World War I and is unusual for an American film in that it is told from the German point of view. The main character, Paul Baumer, is influenced by a college professor to enlist and fight for "the Fatherland." He and his friends are trained by a horrible corporal in boot camp. At the front, Paul meets a soldier, Katczinsky, who helps him cope with the tragedies of war. Eventually Paul loses all his friends and, while reaching for a butterfly, is himself killed.

General Commentary

This has been called one of the finest antiwar films ever made. The realistic battle scenes are hard to forget. Any teacher teaching about World War I and war in general can use this film as a resource. In addition, teachers will find it a great complement to the novel of the same name by Erich Maria Remarque.

Suggested Usage

Previewing Activities

- Students could visit a recruiting center and talk with recruiters about why people enlist in the military.

- Students can collect propaganda from antimilitary and promilitary sources and then discuss the methods each uses to get its point across.

Viewing Activities

GOOD PLACES TO STOP AND TALK

- When the professor is expounding upon the "glory of the fatherland" at the beginning of the film is a good place to stop and talk about the art of persuasion and the role of propaganda. In particular, students can consider the parentalization of countries (e.g., the motherland / the fatherland) in patriotic propaganda techniques.

PATTERNS/STRUCTURES TO LOOK FOR

- The film's early focus on the "glory of the fatherland" is overwhelming. Students can write down the times when they hear that phrase.

- Toward the end of the film there is a tendency to reverse the "glory" idea. Students can note where this change takes place and how often the soldiers talk poorly about the "glory" idea.

Follow-up Activities

- The students can research the effect the movie had on the international community. How did Germany react to the film? What were the responses of other countries?
- The students can read the novel by Erich Maria Remarque and compare and contrast each.
- Using the propaganda material from the previewing activity, the students can debate or discuss which is the more effective—antimilitary or promilitary propaganda.

Other Considerations

None.

Ancillary Material

Remarque, Erich Maria. *All Quiet on the Western Front.* Boston: Little, Brown, 1958.

Rupp, Leila J. *Mobilizing Women for War: German and American Propaganda.* Princeton, N.J.: Princeton University Press, 1978.

An American Tail

Subjects: 3, 5, 18, 20
Playing Time: 81 minutes
Rating: G

Director: Don Bluth
Producer: Steven Spielberg
Date: 1986
Voices of: Phillip Glasser, Dom Deluise, Christopher Plummer

Plot Summary

Fievel Mousekewitz and his family live and suffer in Russia and dream of America. They decide to emigrate and during the voyage, Fievel is thrown overboard. His parents and family assume that he has died, but Fievel is lucky and enters New York harbor in a glass bottle. Meanwhile, his family goes through "mouse immigration" and settles in New York. During his efforts to find his family, Fievel learns that America is not exactly the dreamland his father thought it was. He meets scam artists, sweatshop bosses, and cats! He becomes involved with a political movement organized in part by an Irish mouse political boss to stand up to and drive away the cats. The movement is successful, but, in the meantime, Fievel meets a good cat whom he befriends. Fievel is eventually reunited with his family and begins his life in the United States.

General Commentary

This is an animated version of the traditional European immigrant experience. The father has unrealistic dreams of the United States ("There are no cats in America and all the streets are paved in cheese"). Fievel and his family find out that there are problems in America. The difference is that in America they have the power to overcome their problems. Once Fievel is in America he meets people from all over the world. He is naive about what America has to offer. He is taken advantage of by scam artists and a sweatshop boss. But Fievel also meets idealistic new immigrants, such as the French bird who is helping to build the Statue of Liberty and tells Fievel, "Never say never again"; and the young Irish immigrant who wants to start a union of mice against cats. This movie can be used with ESL and secondary students studying the East Coast immigrant experience.

Suggested Usage

Previewing Activities

- Students can interview immigrants about what they thought America would be like before they arrived and what they discovered America to be.

- Students can research what types of people came to America in 1885 (the year Fievel comes to America) through the port of New York (Ellis Island).

Viewing Activities

Good Places to Stop and Talk

- At the beginning of the movie, the father tells his children what America is like. ESL students can listen to this scene carefully since it sets up a major premise of the movie: the father's unrealistic dreams of America.

- An ESL teacher can use the many visual scenes in this movie as the basis of paired narration activities.

PATTERNS/STRUCTURES TO LOOK FOR

- A number of scenes involve a lot of repetition that an ESL teacher can use to teach different structures. For example, when Fievel and his father are walking up the rope to the ship, Fievel keeps saying "look . . . is that . . . ?" and his father answers "Yes, keep walking."
- Students can keep track of the different images of America and immigrants that are presented in the movie.

Follow-up Activities

- ESL students can research and report on the different topics presented in the film. Possible topics include: the building of the Statue of Liberty, the creation of labor unions, immigrant sweat-shops, Ellis Island, the American spirit, immigrants in the late 1800s, reasons for immigration, and ethnic communities in New York.
- Students can research and report on how today's immigrant experience differs from that of the late 1800s.
- Teachers can lead a discussion on the meaning of the two important metaphors in this film: "There are no cats in America, and the streets are paved with cheese."

Other Considerations

None.

Ancillary Material

Bolino, August C. *The Ellis Island Source Book.* Washington, D.C.: Kensington Historical Press, 1985.

The Andromeda Strain

Subject:	26	**Director:**	Robert Wise
Playing Time:	130 minutes	**Producer:**	Robert Wise
Rating:	G	**Date:**	1971
		Actors:	Arthur Hill, Kate Reid, David Wayne, James Olson

Plot Summary

Two men looking for a downed satellite in the wilds of New Mexico stumble upon the tiny town of Piedmont, where almost all of the 68 inhabitants are dead, victims of a mysterious ailment that turned their blood to powder. The two men soon stop transmitting to their central command, and in a matter of hours a team of scientists has been mobilized to find out why. Several floors below the surface of the earth in a super-secret research station, they scrutinize the satellite and the two survivors of the town, an old man and a baby, for some clue to what overtook the inhabitants of Piedmont. They isolate "Andromeda," an alien organism brought back by the satellite, which when exposed to air, kills humans by crystallizing their blood. As they seek to find the reason why the organism spared the two survivors, they face a deadly leak that brings the research unit within seconds of self-destruction.

General Commentary

Little surpasses this movie for sheer suspense and horror. The opening scenes in Piedmont are terrifying, and the sight of the relatively innocuous "Andromeda" pulsating on the satellite will probably make most viewers want to declare chemical warfare on their front lawns. But what makes it most horrific is the fact that it all seems so plausible—a hallmark feature of author Michael Crichton, who wrote the book on which this story is based. This is an excellent film for for all grades from junior high school through college, and it would also be excellent for ESL students.

Suggested Usage

Previewing Activities

- Students can read *The Andromeda Strain* for purposes of comparison with the movie.
- Students can research some of the different space probes to learn about what has been brought back to earth.
- Students can research the U.S. military's germ / biological warfare technology and report on it.

Viewing Activities

• Teachers may wish to stop the film and have students discuss what they think may have happened after these scenes:

> the scene in which the two men who initially locate Piedmont lose radio contact
>
> the scene in which the airplane flies over Piedmont and sees the dead bodies
>
> the scene in which the old man approaches the scientist in Piedmont

Any of these scenes would also be excellent for paired / reported / mute narrations in ESL classes.

Patterns/Structures to Look For

• This is a movie about a germ named "Andromeda." It might help students, especially those with limited scientific backgrounds, to try to track all the information they learn about "Andromeda" and produce a synthesis of this information. Teachers can assist by stopping the tape after each scene in which new information is presented about "Andromeda."

Follow-up Activities

• The students can compare the book and the movie, either orally or in writing.

• Students can research major germ / chemical leaks that have occurred and report on them.

• Students can research mysterious diseases, such as that which struck the Navajo reservation in the spring of 1993, and report on the possible origins of these diseases.

• As a creative writing project, students can write "the rest of the story," telling what happened to "Andromeda" after the movie left off.

Other Considerations

None.

Ancillary Material

Crichton, Michael. *The Andromeda Strain.* New York: Alfred A. Knopf, 1969.

Annie Hall

Subjects:	4, 9, 13, 27	**Director:**	Woody Allen
Playing Time:	94 minutes	**Producer:**	Charles Jesse
Rating:	PG	**Date:**	1977
		Actors:	Woody Allen, Diane Keaton, Shelley Duvall, Christopher Walken, Colleen Dewhurst, Paul Simon

Plot Summary

This is the story of a romance that doesn't last. Told in flashback by Woody, it details his meeting Annie Hall, a small-town girl living in New York, their romance, and the eventual end of the romance, against the backdrop of New York City in the late 1970s.

General Commentary

The movie recreates the mood of New York at the height of the "me" era. People have intense experiences with analysis, psychobabble is a sort of second dialect, and introspection is an art form. Every interpersonal scene involves an intense fear of personal commitment, which eventually destroys Woody and Annie's relationship. Yet the movie is presented with such a wry twist that one is left with the idea that it is as much a parody as a portrayal. Any class from a mature secondary class and above could use this film.

Suggested Usage

Previewing Activities

- Teachers should consider having students do selected readings on the psychological profile of the "me" generation.
- Selected readings from D. Tannen's *You Just Don't Understand* can also enhance a viewer's appreciation of the breakdown in communication between Woody and Annie.

Viewing Activities

Good Places to Stop and Talk

- Because the film is told in a disjointed flashback style, when working with ESL students it is a good idea to stop the film periodically to have students summarize what they have learned so far about Woody and Annie.
- It would be a shame for ESL students to miss several classic one-liners. In one scene Woody's first wife says, "I love being reduced to a cultural stereotype," and in another Woody complains about how conversations always go back to the subject of Jews. He cites examples where the word "Jew" is confused with the reduction for "did/do you." These scenes can be played and replayed to ensure that students understand the nuances.

- The rooftop scene in which Annie and Woody are talking and subtitles explain what they are really thinking is another great scene that should be reviewed.

PATTERNS/STRUCTURES TO LOOK FOR

- Many scenes can be analyzed for what is really being said. These scenes include the following:

    Woody meeting Annie at the tennis club

    Woody having dinner with Annie's family

    Woody trying to dissuade Annie from moving in with him

    Woody and Annie discussing her use of marijuana.

Follow-up Activities

- The film lends itself to a discussion of whether men and women can / should remain friends after the romance is gone.

- Several fundamental comparisons drawn in the film can be discussed: what men want in a relationship / what women want; big city people / small town people; East Coast life / West Coast life; and Jewish / Protestant outlooks.

- The scenes in which the characters say one thing and mean another can be exploited into spin-off role plays for ESL students.

Other Considerations

There is a lot of sex in this movie. The actual portrayal of sex is limited and there is no nudity, but sex is an ongoing topic of discussion. Furthermore, even with stopping and reviewing the film, it is unlikely that many ESL students will be able to appreciate its sophisticated humor. Nevertheless, its many redeeming qualities make it appropriate for use with ESL students.

Ancillary Material

Hougan, James. *Decadence: Radical Nostalgia, Narcissism and Decline in the Seventies.* New York: William Morrow, 1975.

Tannen, Deborah. *You Just Don't Understand.* New York: William Morrow, 1990.

Apocalypse Now

Subjects:	17, 18, 19, 28	**Director:**	Francis Ford Coppola
Playing Time:	139 minutes	**Producer:**	Francis Ford Coppola
Rating:	R	**Date:**	1979
		Actors:	Martin Sheen, Marlon Brando, Dennis Hopper, Robert Duval, Frederick Forrest

Plot Summary

This drama takes place sometime late in the 1960s or early in the 1970s. It tells of Captain Willard's journey up a river in Vietnam and Cambodia to find a renegade American, Colonel Kurtz, who according to U.S. intelligence officials, has gone mad. Captain Willard's mission is to "terminate" the colonel "with extreme prejudice." Captain Willard is accompanied by three young American soldiers and one older African-American soldier, who is in command of the small boat. As Willard journeys up the river he reads the dossier on Kurtz and confronts the madness that surrounds him. As he gets closer to Kurtz's headquarters, the insanity around him intensifies. The boat is attacked by unseen people, and one young soldier dies. Later the boat is attacked with bows and arrows, and finally the soldier in charge of the boat is struck in the heart by a spear, after which he dies trying to strangle Willard. With the two remaining soldiers, Willard makes it to Kurtz's horrifying headquarters, where he is terrorized by Kurtz. The Chef, one of the two soldiers, is decapitated, and his head is thrown on Willard's lap while Willard is chained up. After Kurtz sets Willard free, Willard decapitates him. Willard leaves with the surviving American soldier, who has been on LSD for most of the journey.

General Commentary

This movie is an excellent choice if you are teaching about America's involvement in Southeast Asia and/or metaphor. The film can be seen as an extended metaphor of one man's journey into madness, and in this case the madness is either Kurtz or America's involvement in Vietnam. The movie can be used with any group of students studying either of these subjects. The director, Coppola, has said that the movie is based on Joseph's Conrad's short story "Heart of Darkness."

Suggested Usage

Previewing Activities

- Students can read Conrad's "Heart of Darkness" before or after viewing the film. Franklin Walker's introduction in the Bantam Classic edition is useful because it examines the symbolism in the story, some of which is evident in the film.

- Students can study the geography of Vietnam and Cambodia and the different types of native peoples who live in those regions.

- Students can research America's involvement in Vietnam and Cambodia.

- Teachers might want to introduce the idea of simile and metaphor because Willard uses an incredible number of similes as he is narrating. Further, the movie itself can be seen as suggesting that Willard's personal journey is a metaphor for America's journey into the madness of the Vietnam War.
- Teachers might have students look up the meaning of the word *apocalypse* and discuss some of the traditional Western interpretations of the Apocalypse in the Bible.
- Teachers might lead a discussion on what napalm is and how it was used during the Vietnam War.

Viewing Activities

GOOD PLACES TO STOP AND TALK

- The second scene in the movie takes place in a military trailer. In this scene Kurtz is introduced and Willard receives his mission. Because this scene is critical for comprehension, ESL teachers might want to do a comprehension check after it.

PATTERNS/STRUCTURES TO LOOK FOR

- Students can keep track of all the insanity that Willard encounters as he goes up the river. This is a partial list of possibilities:

    the wildness of the jungle (a tiger chases Willard and Chef)

    the lunacy of Lieutenant Colonel Kilgore, who puts playing cards on every dead Viet Cong soldier he and his troops kill, who blasts Wagner from his helicopters as he attacks Vietnamese villages, who holds surfing competitions in rivers that are under bombing attacks, and who states that he "loves the smell of napalm in the morning"

    the craziness of an absurd USO show with Playboy playmates dressed as Indians and cowboys in the middle of a war zone

    the massacre of innocent civilians by frightened American soldiers

    the almost surreal experience of arriving at a battle zone where some of the mostly black soldiers think Willard (who has just arrived) is their commanding officer

Follow-up Activities

- Students can discuss or write about the symbolism in the movie, for example: (a) how Willard's journey relates to America's involvement in Vietnam, (b) what Kurtz symbolizes, (c) what the movie is saying when the only other soldier who survives is on drugs throughout the journey, and (d) how the movie presents a vision of the Apocalypse.
- Students can compare and contrast the movie with Conrad's short story.

Other Considerations

This movie contains vulgar language, much graphic violence, one scene of highly suggestive dancing, and a lot of racist names for Vietnamese.

Ancillary Material

Conrad, Joseph. *Heart of Darkness: An Authoritative Text, Backgrounds and Sources, Criticism.* New York: W.W. Norton, 1971.

Hearts of Darkness. Directed by Fax Bahr. Paramount, 1991 (a documentary on the making of *Apocalypse Now*).

Baby Boom

Subjects: 4, 9, 13, 25, 27
Playing Time: 103 minutes
Rating: PG

Director: Charles Shyer
Producer: Nancy Myers
Date: 1987
Actors: Diane Keaton, Sam Shepard

Plot Summary

JC is a yuppie with a career-track mind, an Ivy-league education, a live-in boyfriend, and an upwardly mobile outlook. When she inherits a baby from a distant relative, she explores the adoption option, only to find that she cannot give up the baby. So, she tries to add this new factor into her busy life. Her boyfriend moves out, her boss replaces her on an important account, and she loses everything but her bank account and the baby. Undaunted, she moves to Vermont, where she soon realizes that she will also need to find a way to live, since the bank account is rapidly dwindling. So, she starts a gourmet baby food business. Finally, she has it all: a career, a baby, her own business, a house in the country, and a new boyfriend—the local veterinarian. Then the company she used to work for offers to buy her business. She's tempted, but she realizes that she has it all and "the rat race will have to do with one less rat."

General Commentary

Realistic this movie is not. Its primary value is its lack of realism. It can be reduced to the following formula: woman has it all; woman gets a baby; woman still has it all (only in a different way). This is a very funny movie that works well because it is such a parody of the way things really are. It makes an excellent vehicle for discussion of stereotypes and images.

Suggested Usage

Previewing Activities

- ESL teachers may wish to acquaint their students with the word "yuppie" and preteach a little about the meaning of the word and the profile of the type of person the word evokes.

- All types of students can analyze the role of women in fairy tales. Most such tales can be reduced to the following analysis: woman leads a charmed life; woman experiences difficulties from outside forces; woman surmounts difficulties and goes on to lead a charmed life (happily ever after) in a different venue. A discussion of how fairy tale images shaped the lives of women in the past might also be appropriate.

Viewing Activities

GOOD PLACES TO STOP AND TALK

- ESL teachers may wish to stop to check for comprehension after the scene in which JC has dinner with her boss, and the scene in which JC meets her boyfriend at the train.

- If students are properly primed to analyze fairy tales, teachers can have them look for features of fairy tales in this story. Apart from the above-mentioned structure, they can look for the ineffectual man (often the father), the wicked witch, the fairy godmother, and Prince Charming.
- A stereotype of American business is also developed in this movie. Students can look for the features of business that are shown in the movie.

Follow-up Activities

- Students can analyze the movie for the components of a fairy tale.
- Students can compare what this movie says about family values and parenting with another "parenting" movie, such as *Three Men and a Baby*.
- Students can develop the images of business shown in this movie and then write a response to those images.
- Students can read the critique of *Baby Boom* in the book *Backlash*.

Other Considerations

Off-camera sex is implied in two scenes.

Ancillary Material

Faludi, Susan. *Backlash: The Undeclared War Against American Women*. New York: Crown, 1991.

The Ballad of Gregorio Cortez

Subjects: 3, 16, 23, 29
Playing Time: 94 minutes
Rating: PG

Director: Robert M. Young
Producers: Moctesuma Esparza and Michael Hausman
Date: 1983
Actors: Edward J. Olmos, Robert Gammon

Plot Summary

In 1901, a young Mexican cow-hand accidentally shot a sheriff in a dispute caused by the sheriff's mistranslation of a word. A two-week manhunt ensued that involved the Texas Rangers. Gregorio Cortez was eventually caught, only a few feet away from Mexico, and brought to trial. He spent 12 years in jail. The high point of the film comes at the end, when, awaiting trial, the translation error is explained to him.

General Commentary

This true story is an excellent movie for students of all ages and backgrounds to see. It is a period piece, and the time and the mood, particularly the attitudes of Anglos and Mexicans toward each other, are well captured. No movie could better show the plight of non-English-speaking persons in the hands of an English-only legal system. The events of this movie may have happened almost 100 years ago, but the issue of legal rights of non-English-speaking people is still current.

Suggested Usage

Previewing Activities

- Students could find and listen to the Mexican border song about this incident. It would be necessary to provide non-Spanish speakers with a translation, since the song is in Spanish.

- A class might benefit from a visit by a policeperson to explain the Miranda rights and from library research about subsequent Supreme Court rulings on the use of languages other than English in giving the Miranda rights. If possible, a teacher could obtain foreign language versions of the rights from the local police station.

Viewing Activities

GOOD PLACES TO STOP AND TALK

- It's an excellent idea to do a comprehension check after the scene in which Cortez shoots the sheriff and after the scene in which Cortez talks to the translator while he is awaiting arraignment.

PATTERNS/STRUCTURES TO LOOK FOR

- Students can consider the different attitudes that people have toward Gregorio Cortez: the sheriff, his family, the people he meets as he runs away, and the translator.

Follow-Up Activities

- Students can do library research to learn more about the manhunt for Gregorio Cortez.
- Students may wish to investigate famous legal cases involving foreign nationals or non-English-speaking persons. Some examples might be the cases of Sirhan Sirhan (who shot Robert Kennedy) and Bruno Hauptman (of the Lindbergh kidnapping case—see also *Murder on the Orient Express*.)

Other Considerations

The film is shot in English, Spanish, and Tex-Mex, but there are no subtitles, so viewers will not understand the crux until the end, unless they speak Spanish.

Belizaire, the Cajun

Subjects:	3, 4, 13, 16, 24	**Director:**	Glen Pitre
Playing Time:	113 minutes	**Producer:**	Howard Shore
Rating:	PG	**Date:**	1985
		Actors:	Armand Assante, Gail Young

Plot Summary

A Cajun folk healer, Belizaire, lives in southwest Louisiana in 1855. Belizaire and his cousin Polit and many other Cajuns are threatened with exile by night-riding vigilantes who want them to leave. Many are planning to go to Texas. Belizaire is in love with Alida, a Cajun woman in a semi-morganatic marriage with Mathew Perry, the son of a powerful, non-Cajun landowner, who rides with the vigilantes. One day, Mathew Perry turns up dead and the suspect is Polit. To save Polit, whom Belizaire knows cannot have committed the crime, Belizaire confesses to the crime. Polit is killed by the vigilantes anyway. Now Belizaire must face the gallows for a crime he didn't commit, but he brings a new brand of gallows humor to the execution, and using his own charm and a bit of backwoods superstition, forces the real murderer to identify himself. Belizaire is now free to pursue Alida.

General Commentary

Perhaps because this film introduces the viewer to a region and an ethnic group that are not often shown in movies, the film has an almost foreign flavor. The lilting Acadian English, occasionally interspersed with Acadian French, and the roguish exploits of the main character, who can con anyone from the local priest to the murderer, suggest a subtitle: *The Exploits of a Cajun Operator*. It is an excellent movie to use to introduce students of all ages to the culture of the Cajuns; however, because of the relative authenticity of the speech, care should be taken in introducing this movie to ESL students.

Suggested Usage

Previewing Activities

- A printed text that rolls at the beginning of the movie tells a little bit about the history of the Cajuns. Teachers could use this text as a springboard from which to develop a social studies unit on the Cajuns. One suggested component might be Longfellow's poem "Evangeline," which gives much of the history of how the Cajuns came to be in Louisiana. With ESL students, the poem could be used for work with oral skills as well as for comprehension of the subject.

- A teacher could supply a map of Cajun country so that references within the movie (going to Texas, going to Galveston) are clear.

- Students who are not familiar with Roman Catholicism could be instructed on the nature of the Catholic concept of confession, which begins and ends this movie.

Bracknell and **Wokingham College**

Viewing Activities

GOOD PLACES TO STOP AND TALK

- Teachers may wish to stop the film for comprehension checks after these scenes:

    Belizaire's discussion with Alida about the nature of her marriage

    the scene in which the vigilantes ride to tell people to leave (this would also make an excellent silent / paired narration in an ESL class)

    the scene in which James and Matthew argue with Mathew's father

    the scene in which James and his sister argue about their inheritance

    the scene in which Belizaire "cuts the deal" to save the life of Polit

PATTERNS/STRUCTURES TO LOOK FOR

- American students could listen for the Cajun accent and the use of French. It is particularly noteworthy that French is used when people are most upset or angry.

Follow-up Activities

- Any of the previewing activities can also be used as a follow-up activity.

- Students can research and report on the Cajuns today. The class can be divided into groups, and each group can be given one of the following assignments to research and report on: the influence of Cajuns in Louisiana politics today; the influence of Cajun cooking on American cooking; the influence of Cajun music on American music; and the influence of Cajun language on American English

Other Considerations

Teachers should be aware that the dialect used in this film requires that the film be given absolute attention while being viewed. There are bedroom scenes, but without sex or nudity.

Ancillary Material

Longfellow, Henry W. *Evangeline: A Tale of Acadie* . . . Boston: B H Sanborn, 1899.

Bob Roberts

Subjects:	4, 22	**Director:**	Tim Robbins
Playing Time:	102 minutes	**Producer:**	Forrest Murray
Rating:	R	**Date:**	1992
		Actors:	Tim Robbins, Gore Vidal

Plot Summary

Bob Roberts is a singer, philosopher, and candidate for the U.S. Senate. He tells it like it is, or at least how he thinks it is. He is conservative, he quotes the *Bible*, and he never has a hair out of place. He is traveling in a bus around Pennsylvania, hammering away at the Democratic incumbent senator. Both candidates face scandals. Bob Roberts is hounded by a reporter who is sure he is connected to a drug-smuggling scheme. In an assassination attempt, Roberts is paralyzed. Or is he? The hounding reporter is blamed, but found innocent.(He is murdered anyway.) Roberts is elected to the Senate in a close vote. Still confined to his wheelchair as a paraplegic, he sings, plays guitar, and taps his toes into the hearts of the Republican party.

General Commentary

This drama-documentary does an outstanding job of satirizing the conservative political agenda of the Republican party in the 1980s. It combines a number of events and issues of the decade, such as the Iran-Contra affair, the conservative religious movement, and the drug smuggling in Central America. Teachers will find this film useful as a resource for teaching about the American political system and satire.

Suggested Usage

Previewing Activities

- Students can investigate some of the political and social differences between Democrats and Republicans.

- Students can interview local politicians about their campaigns.

- Students may want to research the 1980s and the campaigns that took place during that time.

Viewing Activities

GOOD PLACES TO STOP AND TALK

- The scenes where Bob is confronted by the reporter are good places to stop and discuss what is happening. Students can answer the following questions:

    What accusations is the reporter making against Bob?

    Were they actual events that took place?

- The scene where the mother and her sons speak to Bob may be used to discuss what type of people would follow Bob Roberts.

- The songs that Bob plays throughout the movie have strong messages. The students can listen to the songs and write down what they think the messages are.

Follow-up Activities

- Students can go through old newspapers and find articles on politicians and their campaigns.
- Students may research politicians who have been assassinated or who have suffered an assassination attempt (such as George Wallace).
- Students can write a satire or create a series of political cartoons depicting politicians running for office.

Other Considerations

Although this film deals with high-level satire, there are no sex scenes and very little profanity. It's hard to believe it received an "R" rating.

Ancillary Material

Scott, Peter Dale, Paul L. Hoch, and Rusell Stetler. *The Assassinations: Dallas and Beyond: A Guide to Cover-ups and Investigations*. New York: Random House, 1976.

The Bounty

Subjects:	1, 7, 14, 17, 23, 31	**Director:**	Roger Donaldson
Playing Time:	130 minutes	**Producer:**	Bernard Williams
Rating:	PG	**Date:**	1984
		Actors:	Mel Gibson, Anthony Hopkins, Laurence Olivier, Daniel Day Lewis

Plot Summary

This is a retelling of the mutiny on HMS *Bounty* in the 1700s. It is told in a series of flashbacks by Captain Bligh as he is questioned by a naval review board in London about the events of the mutiny near Polynesia. The story starts with the preparations of the *Bounty* to go to Fiji in search of breadfruit plants, details the events of the voyage, the sojourn in Tahiti, and the subsequent mutiny, culminating with the trip by the mutineers under the leadership of Fletcher Christian to Pitcairn's Island.

General Commentary

This lush, beautifully filmed movie is an attempt to explain the psychological forces that caused the mutiny to happen. It is a movie caught between cross-purposes: it can't decide whether it should be a highly visual travel-adventure film or a dark and brooding psychological drama. It does far better as the former.

Suggested Usage

Previewing Activities

- This movie is not based on the classic *Mutiny on the Bounty* of the Bounty trilogy by Nordhoff-Hall. Even so, students could read the book for purposes of general schema building and for eventual comparison between the movie and the book.

- Students can do map work to trace the route of the *Bounty* from England, around the Horn, to the South Seas, and eventually to Pitcairn's Island.

- Students could research a variety of topics to build schema to watch the movie. Encyclopedia topics to consider include the mutiny on the *Bounty*, Fletcher Christian, Captain William Bligh, Pitcairn's Island, and breadfruit. There is also extensive reference to Captain Cook in this movie. His life could also be researched. Students could also research the maritime laws pertaining to mutiny.

Viewing Activities

GOOD PLACES TO STOP AND TALK

- ESL teachers could use several excellent sea scenes for paired narrations, including the trip around the Horn and the entry into Tahiti.

- Certain scenes are critical to understanding the movie, and none more than the first scene in which Bligh describes the proposed trip to Fletcher Christian, and the scene in which the actual mutiny takes place and Christian decides to set Bligh adrift rather than kill him. These are good places to check for comprehension.

- An interesting pattern to look for is the differences in the reactions of Bligh and Christian to the following situations:

  the mission of the Bounty

  the dangers going around the Horn

  the beauty of Polynesia

  the meetings with Polynesians

Follow-up Activities

- The movie leaves the viewer with several questions about why people behaved the way they did. A discussion exploring the reasons for Bligh and Christian's behavior is strongly recommended.
- Students might compare the books listed in the previewing activities and the movie.
- Students might research the subsequent history of Pitcairn's Island and the descendants of the mutineers. In particular, they can read *Pitcairn's Island*, which is part of the Bounty trilogy by Nordhoff-Hall. A report on the island's history and its position today could be a follow-up project.

Activities for Low-Level ESL Students

The following activities are suggested for use with low-level ESL students. A teacher can:

- play the scene in which Captain Bligh describes the forthcoming trip to Fletcher Christian. First play the scene without sound so that students can see the facial expressions of each man. Then play the scene as a modified cloze passage, in which some students listen for missing parts of Bligh's speech and some listen for missing parts of Christian's speech. Ask the students how each man feels about the forthcoming trip.
- (midway through the trip to Tahiti, after the trip around the Horn) have the students choose different characters (Christian, Bligh, various sailors). The students can write journal entries in which they report on the trip thus far from their chosen character's point of view and then share these with the class.
- have students plot the trip on a map of the world. As each new place is mentioned, have a student find the location on the map.
- do the entry into Tahiti scene as a paired narration.
- write a cloze passage of the scene in which Christian and Bligh plan to get around the problem of the woman who expects to sleep with Bligh. Discuss the custom and the reactions of the two men to the custom.
- play the actual mutiny scene and stop immediately afterward. Assign some students to explain why some sailors went with Bligh and other students to explain why some sailors stayed with Christian.

Other Considerations

A few scenes of appropriate nudity are a logical consequence of the South Seas setting of the movie.

Ancillary Material

Nordhoff, Charles, and James Norman Hall. *The Bounty Trilogy: Comprising the Three Volumes Mutiny on the Bounty, Men Against the Sea*, and *Pitcairn's Island*. Boston: Little, Brown, 1951.

Boyz 'N the Hood

Subjects:	2, 4, 10, 11, 13, 23	**Director:**	John Singleton
Playing Time:	111 minutes	**Producer:**	Steve Nicolaides
Rating:	R	**Date:**	1991
		Actors:	Lawrence Fishburne, Ice Cube, Cuba Gooding, Jr., Morris Chestnut

Plot Summary

The background for this compelling drama is south-central Los Angeles in the mid-1980s. Three African-American boys, Tre, Ricky, and Doughboy, are friends living across the street from each other. Tre and Ricky are very close. They share their dreams with each other. We find out that Ricky wants to play football at USC and Tre wants to get married and go to college. Doughboy, on the other hand, is the leader of a group of angry neighborhood boys who are constantly in trouble. The film follows their last year in high school and the trials and tragedy that are part of the "hood."

General Commentary

This outstanding film captures the real-life issues of urban African-American youth. The film ends with the message "increase the peace"; ironically, it caused a great deal of violence at the theaters. Nonetheless, this film is excellent to use in a class examining American social problems, American minorities, violence and crime, and urban America.

Suggested Usage

Previewing Activities

• Students may want to view the footage of the riots that took place after the Rodney King incident since this is where the story takes place. Students who did not see the actual Rodney King tape may wish to view the first scene of *Malcolm X*.

• Students can cut out articles on gang crime and behavior in their city to read and become familiar with the type of activities gangs engage in.

Viewing Activities

GOOD PLACES TO STOP AND TALK

• The scene where the house is broken into and Tre and his father sit down and talk would be a good place to have a discussion on the effects of crime on innocent people.

PATTERNS/STRUCTURES TO LOOK FOR

• The behavior of each of the main characters is a clue to his future. Teachers might have students keep track of the behavior and discuss the results of it.

Follow-up Activities

- Secondary students could put on a gang-awareness assembly.
- Students can study the crime rates of inner-city areas and compare them to other areas. Students can also speculate on the result of the comparison
- Students can write about or discuss how segregation still exists in the United States.
- Students can examine the three main characters and write a short biography of each.
- Teachers may want to have students research, report on, and discuss the controversy that surrounded this film when it was first released.

Other Considerations

The language used in the film may be offensive to some students. There is one gratuitous sex scene.

Ancillary Material

Hinton, S.E. *The Outsiders*. New York: Dell Publishing, 1967.

Breaker Morant

Subjects: 14, 19
Playing Time: 107 Minutes
Rating: R

Director: Bruce Beresford
Producer: Matt Carroll
Date: 1981
Actors: Edward Woodward, Jack Thompson, John Waters

Plot Summary

This true story depicts the court-martial of Lt. Harry "Breaker" Morant, an Australian lieutenant fighting with the British against the Boers (Dutch colonists) in 1901 in South Africa's Boer Wars. Although the Boers had been there long before, the British were intent on securing certain territory for themselves. British orders at the time were to shoot all Boer prisoners, which Morant does. Much to his surprise he and two other lieutenants are arrested after executing prisoners. They are court-martialed. During the trial, it is clear that the British need to convict the three for other purposes. The film ends with the execution of poet and soldier, "Breaker" Morant.

General Commentary

This film won ten awards from the Australian Academy. This courtroom drama could be used across disciplines. ESL students would find the courtroom dialogue helpful in understanding questioning styles. Any teacher may want to use the film as an introduction to the Boer War or as a way to discuss a particular aspect of South African history.

Suggested Usage

Previewing Activities

• The students can define the term *imperialism*.

• The students could research the British Empire and create a map identifying those countries that became colonies of Britain.

• The teacher may want to do the previous exercise with other Western powers.

• Students could research the Boer War and report on it.

Viewing Activities

GOOD PLACES TO STOP AND TALK

• The courtroom scenes where the defense lawyer is questioning the judges and asking that the case be thrown out are excellent places for the teacher to ask the students if Morant and the men are being treated fairly, and why or why not.

• The teacher may want to stop the film just after the Boers attack the fort where Morant is imprisoned. The teacher may ask the students to speculate whether this act of heroism may help Morant and the others' case.

Bracknell and Wokingham College

Patterns/Structures to Look For

- ESL teachers may want to have the students take note of the questioning technique that is used by the lawyers on both sides.

Follow-up Activities

- Some students can research the event in newspapers or other reference materials.

- Students could perform a mock trial of the case to retry the lieutenants. This kind of activity is highly recommended for ESL students.

- Students could write an obituary of "Breaker" Morant or one of the other lieutenants.

Other Considerations

None.

Bugsy

Subjects: 3, 4, 7, 11
Playing Time: 135 minutes
Rating: R

Director: Barry Levinson
Producers: Mark Johnson, Barry Levinson, and Warren Beatty
Date: 1991
Actors: Warren Beatty, Annette Bening, Ben Kingsley, Elliot Gould

Plot Summary

During World War II Benjamin "Bugsy" Siegel, an East Coast gangster, "branched out" to the West Coast and eventually developed the first casino in Las Vegas—the Flamingo. The movie begins with his original trip west and continues with his meeting Virginia Hill, another mobster's girlfriend, who was to become the one true passion of his life. The movie then depicts the building of the Flamingo and Bugsy's efforts to get financial backing for his dream project. His two passions, the Flamingo and Virginia Hill, intersected when Virginia stole money from the Flamingo building funds, which eventually brought down the wrath and retribution of the mob upon Bugsy.

General Commentary

This is not so much a movie about the development of Las Vegas as it is a portrait of a gangster with Graham Greene-esque overtones. Benjamin Siegel is portrayed as the riddle he was: a Jewish member of a mostly Italian Catholic underworld; a family man who went to great lengths to protect his wife and children, but set a new standard in philandering; a nice guy from the old neighborhood who was nevertheless capable of blowing away a friend who had "talked" to the FBI; and a politically aware Jewish male who, in the midst of World War II, wanted nothing so much as to assassinate Mussolini. Above all, it is the story of a person who wanted to be better than he was and who would do anything, including murder, to get what he wanted. It's definitely a "heavy" movie, and one that would be suitable only for use with college students, very advanced high school students, and very advanced ESL students.

Suggested Usage

Previewing Activities

This is an excellent movie for focussing on organized crime in America and the role that Las Vegas and the state of Nevada play in that organization. A teacher may wish to have students do any or all of the following as previewing activities.

- Investigate the lives of Bugsy Siegel and Virginia Hill from newspaper accounts. These can be used later for comparison / contrast. Obituaries may be of particular use in getting solid information for students to use.

- Research the history of legalized gambling in America, including gambling in Las Vegas and in Atlantic City, and in lotteries and on Indian reservations.

- Research the history of Las Vegas. Write to the Chamber of Commerce and ask for information about the history of legalized gambling and casinos in Las Vegas.

Viewing Activities

GOOD PLACES TO STOP AND TALK

- A few scenes are critical for the comprehension of the movie. The following are good places to stop to do comprehension checks:

    after Bugsy kills the man to whom he gave a shirt

    after Bugsy buys his house in Los Angeles

    after Bugsy and Virginia visit Las Vegas the first time

    after Bugsy explains his "dream" to the mobsters at his daughter's party

PATTERNS/STRUCTURES TO LOOK FOR

- Most exploitable is the portrait of the man himself. The teacher may wish to have different students "track" different aspects of his character for purposes of follow-up discussion. In particular, students may be directed to focus on Bugsy as a family man, a Jew, a lover, a businessman, a killer, and a friend.

Follow-up Activities

- If students were directed to find newspaper accounts about Bugsy and Virginia Hill as part of the previewing activities, they may be directed to compare those facts with the movie version.

- The teacher can lead a discussion in which students give their opinions about the different aspects of Bugsy's personality, using examples from the movie.

- Students might be directed to do library research about the subsequent history of the Flamingo casino and how gambling is a part of the economy of the state of Nevada.

Other Considerations

There are several "sexual" scenes, but no nudity, and several scenes of intense physical violence.

Butch Cassidy and the Sundance Kid

Subjects: 1, 3, 7, 16, 29, 31
Playing Time: 112 minutes
Rating: PG

Director: George Roy Hill
Producer: John Foreman
Date: 1969
Actors: Paul Newman, Robert Redford, Katherine Ross

Plot Summary

Butch Cassidy and the Sundance Kid were two likeable outlaws in the old West. This movie traces their lives and robbery exploits with the Hole in the Wall Gang, their relentless pursuit by a posse, and their retreat to Bolivia, where they continued their criminal activities and were finally killed by the Bolivian army.

General Commentary

This is a great film to use as an introduction to legends of the old West and gangs. It is appropriate for all levels of students: secondary, college, and ESL. It is especially recommended for ESL students for several reasons. First, the dialogue is clear and understandable. Second, the movie is very visual and has lots of non-speaking sections. Finally, the story is truly an American legend.

Suggested Usage

Previewing Activities

• Students can research gangs in the old West.

• Students can research Butch Cassidy, the Sundance Kid, and the Hole in the Wall Gang. A map exercise, which shows where they operated, can be included.

Viewing Activities

GOOD PLACES TO STOP AND TALK

• For ESL teachers, many self-contained scenes (such as the bedroom scene and the failed bankrobbing scene) can be clipped out to use for paired narration or focused listening (especially for questions and answers, since Newman and Redford ask each other questions in many scenes). An example of a question-and-answer scene is the scene where Butch and Sundance are discussing what they should do to get away from the posse.

• After Butch and Sundance jump off the cliff is a good place to stop and ask students to predict what they think might happen.

- This film has a number of scenes in which the two main characters disagree. Examples include the following:

  whether to trust the old man Butch asks to guard them from the posse

  whether to jump off the cliff

  whether it was right to go to Bolivia

  once they are shot, how each should give cover to each other and where they should go next

  Students can be asked to listen for cues that indicate the two characters' disagreement.

Follow-up Activities

- Students can research the theories that explain what happened to Butch Cassidy and the Sundance Kid. Some say they returned to the United States, where they died of old age.

- Students can read or research about the old West.

- Students can read *Coyote Waits* by Tony Hillerman, a murder mystery based in part on a search for what happened to Butch Cassidy.

Activities for Low-Level ESL Students

The following activities are suggested for use with low-level ESL students. A teacher can:

- preteach some of the unusual idioms used in the second scene when Sundance is accused of cheating in a card game (to hit someone, to clean everyone out, to go bust, hell-of-a, to spot, to be short on brotherly love, over-the-hill, to stick around, to draw on someone); have students do a mute viewing of the scene and guess how the vocabulary might be used in the scene; then have them do a focused listening of the scene to answer the following kinds of questions:

  What did the dark-haired man accuse Sundance of?

  What did Sundance and Butch want the man to ask them?

  Describe Butch and Sundance.

- do a mute narration activity of the first train robbery scene.

- do a cloze exercise of the song "Raindrops Keep Falling on My Head" based on rhyming patterns, progressive reductions, and/or contractions. Students can then discuss how the song might relate to the two main characters.

- do a focused listening activity, such as a cloze, of the dialogue between Butch and Sundance after they get rid of one of their horses and right before they realize the posse is still following them. The dialogue is full of non-standard and tag questions.

- do a mute viewing of the scene where Etta, Butch, and Sundance get off the train in Bolivia. Teachers may want to have students guess where they are, and then write dialogue for the scene. The scene is full of very descriptive body language.

- play the scene of the failed bank robbery attempt, up to the point where Etta is giving them a Spanish lesson in how to rob banks in Spanish. Students can then write their own monologue in English on robbing a bank. This is a great review of imperatives and questions (Raise your hands! Where's the money?).

Other Considerations

None.

Ancillary Material

Hillerman, Tony: *Coyote Waits*. New York: Harper & Row, 1992.

Kelly, Charles. *The Outlaw Trail; A History of Butch Cassidy and His Wild Bunch*. New York: Devin-Adair Co., 1959.

Pointer, Larry. *In Search of Butch Cassidy*. Norman: University of Oklahoma Press, 1977.

Camelot

Subjects:	16, 17, 20, 25	**Director:**	Joshua Logan
Playing Time:	178 minutes	**Producer:**	Jack L. Warner
Rating:	G	**Date:**	1967
		Actors:	Richard Harris, David Hemmings, Vanessa Redgrave, Franco Nero

Plot Summary

This musical adaptation of the legend of King Arthur and the knights of the round table begins when Arthur accidentally meets his bride-to-be, Guenevere, in the woods. They get married and fall in love. When Arthur decides to form the fellowship of the Knights of the Round Table, he requests all knights join him. Lancelot arrives in Camelot and quickly becomes a friend of Arthur. Eventually, Lancelot falls in love with Guenevere and they have an affair. The other knights suspect what is going on, but Arthur refuses to acknowledge his wife and best friend's betrayal. Finally, Arthur's illegitimate son shows up and sets up Lancelot and Guenevere one night when Arthur is away from the court. After the affair is exposed, Lancelot flees Camelot and Guenevere is sentenced to be burned at the stake. Arthur is helpless to defend her, but at the last moment Lancelot saves Guenevere. The movie ends with Arthur relieved that Guenevere will not die, Guenevere leaving for a convent in France, and Lancelot and Arthur preparing to fight each other, which neither wants to do.

General Commentary

There are a lot of reasons why a teacher might want to use this movie in a classroom. For ESL students this a great opportunity to learn about the Arthurian legend in Western civilization and all the accompanying cultural schema (e.g., chivalry). The movie is entertaining and very visual, and even today we use metaphors from this legend (such as referring to the Kennedy administration as Camelot, or referring to a heroic and handsome man as a Lancelot). For American secondary students this is also an entertaining and interesting way of examining English mythology.

Suggested Usage

Previewing Activities

- Since there are so many references to the earlier Arthurian legend (such as Merlin and the sword of Excaliber), teachers can preteach the legend by having students read any of the many versions of the legend.

- Students can examine the concept of chivalry, which is central to the story.

- ESL teachers might want to preteach some of the songs in the movie. This is a fun way to work on pronunciation.

Viewing Activities

- ESL teachers might stop after the following places in the movie:

   after the first song, "I Wonder What the King Is Doing Tonight," which sets up who King Arthur is and what he is anticipating

   after Guenevere's song "Where are the Simple Joys of Maidenhood?" which sets up who Guenevere is

   after Lancelot's song "C'est Moi," which sets up who he is

   These might also be good songs to preteach

- The scene where Guenevere sings / prays to her patron saint might also be a good place to stop, because the concept of patron saints might be foreign to some students.

- ESL teachers might want to have students view carefully two conversations critical to comprehension. They are the scene where Arthur is talking to old King Pellenore about the concept of a trial by jury, and Arthur's conversation with Mordred where it is implied that Mordred is Arthur's illegitimate son.

PATTERNS/STRUCTURES TO LOOK FOR

- Since the movie is very long and visually appealing, teachers might want to consider having students write descriptions of the way things look in the movie (how people dress, what rooms look like, what the castle looks like).

Follow-up Activities

- Students can research and report on life in the Middle Ages. Possible research topics include: life at court, clothing, food, banquets, knights, women, common folk, royalty, the system of serfdom, the church, music, law—adultery laws, castles, and furnishings.

- Students can write on what they think Arthur's idea of civilization was and whether he was a man of his times or a man of the future.

- Students can analyze whether Arthur's character can be considered heroic. He seems perfect in many ways except for his one flaw: he trusts people too much—Lancelot, Guenevere, and even Mordred.

- Students can research and report on theories that Camelot was real and not just a legend.

- As an exercise in metaphor extension, teachers might want to have students talk or write about why Americans refer to the Kennedy administration as a Camelot.

Other Considerations

This long movie probably should not be shown in one sitting.

Ancillary Material

Steinbeck, John. *The Acts of King Arthur and His Noble Knights*. New York: Farrar, Straus, and Giroux, 1976.

White, T.H. *The Once and Future King*. New York: Putnam, 1958.

Cocoon

Subjects: 4, 20, 24, 25
Playing Time: 115 minutes
Rating: PG-13

Director: Ron Howard
Producers: Richard D. Zanuck, David Brown, and Lili Fini Zanuck
Date: 1985
Actors: Wilford Brimley, Steve Guttenberg, Brian Dennehy, Hume Cronyn, Don Ameche, Maureen Stapleton, Jessica Tandy, Gwen Verdon, Tanhee Welch

Plot Summary

This story concerns aliens, aging, life and death, and the Fountain of Youth. A group of elderly residents of a retirement home in St. Petersburg, Florida, swim every day in the pool of a deserted mansion. One day they notice large egg-shaped objects on the bottom of the pool. They continue to swim and each day they feel better and younger. Walter, who is leasing the mansion, allows them to continue coming. Eventually, they find out that Walter is an alien and the eggs are cocoons of other aliens. Walter offers the group an opportunity to experience eternal youth. If they accept, they will lose all they have on earth.

General Commentary

This interesting science-fiction comedy looks at a number of "hot" topics in a comic way. Old age and aspiring to look and feel young are current topics that aren't always handled well in movies. The topic of aliens is also one that sparks people's interest. This film can be used for students studying myth, legend, aging, America's preoccupation with youth, and even American history. (Ponce de León searched for the Fountain of Youth in Florida in 1513.)

Suggested Usage

Previewing Activities

- Students might research the biology and sociology (particularly the demographics) of aging. In particular, students can be directed to research where people retire when they get older.

- Students can analyze the images of aging in American popular culture. This may involve listening to songs such as "Mother's Little Helper" by the Rolling Stones ("What a drag it is getting old") or watching TV's *The Golden Girls*, which presents aging in a more positive light.

- Students can research and report on the life and explorations of Ponce de León.

- Students might discuss what they think it might be like to get old and what kind of life they want when they become old.
- ESL students might discuss or report on what it is like to be older in their country.

Viewing Activities

GOOD PLACES TO STOP AND TALK

- The teacher might stop the film at the scene where the elderly folks exit the pool full of cocoons and suddenly feel better. Students can discuss the following kinds of questions: Who first thought there might be a "fountain of youth"? Why do people strive to find eternal youth?

PATTERNS/STRUCTURES TO LOOK FOR

- Students can note the activities of the retirees after they find added energy and compare it to what they did previously.

Follow-up Activities

- Students might go to a retirement home and visit with the elderly.
- Students can write about the kind of life they want to have when they are elderly.
- ESL students might compare the lives of the elderly in their countries with the lives of the elderly in the United States.
- Students may also want to research UFO sightings and report back to the class. Teachers can have the students debate whether UFOs exist.

Other Considerations

None.

Ancillary Material

Vesperi, Maria D. *City of Green Benches: Growing Old in a New Downtown*. Ithaca: Cornell University Press, 1985.

The Color Purple

Subjects: 2, 4, 13, 17, 23, 27
Playing Time: 155 minutes
Rating: PG-13

Director: Steven Spielberg
Producers: Kathleen Kennedy, Frank Marshall, Quincy Jones, and Steven Spielberg
Date: 1985
Actors: Danny Glover, Whoopi Goldberg, Margaret Avery, Oprah Winfrey

Plot Summary

Before she is 15 years old, an African-American women named Celie has two babies by a man whom she thinks is her father. (She learns later that he wasn't her biological father.) When she is 15, she is given away in marriage to Mister, who beats and abuses her. Her sister, Nettie, fearing sexual advances by her father, moves in with Celie and Mister; Nettie soon is kicked out after she refuses to have sex with Mister. The two sisters are separated, and even though Nettie continues to write Celie over the years, her letters never reach Celie because Mister controls the mailbox. There are several subplots. Celie's step-son Harpo marries a strong-willed woman named Sophia, who is eventually destroyed by the white mayor after she talks back to his wife. Shug Avery, Mister's lover, shows up and becomes a friend of Celie. Eventually, Shug and Celie have an affair. Toward the end of the movie, Shug and Celie discover Nettie's letters that Mister has hidden from Celie. She learns that her two children, who were taken from her at birth, were adopted by a minister's family whom Nettie befriended after she was kicked out of Mister's house. Celie also learns that her sister, the minister and his wife, and her children have been living in Africa as missionaries. Celie demands her independence from Mister, and is eventually reunited with her sister and her children.

General Commentary

This very moving story is adapted from Alice Walker's novel of the same name. It is recommended for secondary, ESL, and college-level students. It would be useful for students reading Alice Walker's novel, for those studying about life for African-Americans in the rural South during the first part of this century or about the African-American experience in America in general, and/or for those studying family relations.

Suggested Usage

Previewing Activities

• Students can read Alice Walker's book.

• Students can research what life was like in the rural South for African-Americans during the early part of this century.

• Teachers, especially ESL teachers, might want to have students listen to some blues and gospel music, both of which are sung in this movie.

Viewing Activities

GOOD PLACES TO STOP AND TALK

- The scene after Sophia is let out of prison and is forced to work for the mayor's wife is a good place to stop and talk about why Sophia's actions were so bold for the time and place she lived.

- Teachers might also want to stop after the scene in which the mayor's wife thinks she has been attacked by the African-American men. This scene demonstrates the basic distrust and misunderstanding white people had of African-Americans in the South.

PATTERNS/STRUCTURES TO LOOK FOR

- Students can be asked to focus on how the women Celie meets (Nettie, Sophia, Shug) affect her life and how the men in her life (her father and Mister) affect her.

- Students can keep track of the events they think are important in changing Celie's life.

Follow-up Activities

- Students can write about or discuss the movie's contradictory images, including the dominating African-American men and powerful African-American women; the jutjoint society and the church-going society; and dysfunctional families and well-adjusted families.

- Students can write on the position of women in this movie.

- Students can research and report on the back-to-Africa movement alluded to in this film.

Other Considerations

Some students could develop an inaccurate stereotype of African-American men if the movie and its characters are not put in proper perspective. One very mild lesbian love scene might dissuade secondary teachers from using the film. Also, there are some very violent scenes.

Ancillary Material

Walker, Alice. *The Color Purple*. New York: Harcourt, Brace, Jovanovich, 1982.

Come See the Paradise

Subjects: 3, 4, 6, 13, 22, 23, 25 **Director:** Alan Parker
Playing Time: 138 minutes **Producer:** Robert F. Colesberry
Rating: R **Date:** 1990
 Actors: Dennis Quaid, Tamlyn Tomita

Plot Summary

The Kawamura family, a family of Issei (first-generation Japanese immigrants) and Nisei (second-generation Japanese-Americans) from Los Angeles are caught up in the relocation and incarceration of Japanese-Americans in internment camps during World War II. The story starts when Jack, a Caucasian, goes to work as a movie projectionist at the Kawamura's theater, and progresses through his romance and elopement with Lilly Kawamura, their return to Los Angeles on the eve of the internment, and their separation in the war, as Lilly stays at Manzanar with their child and Jack is sent off with the military. The movie ends with their reunion at the end of the war.

General Commentary

This is a beautiful movie, a softly burnished period piece that evokes in lasting images the life of the Japanese-Americans before the internment. It is a simple, straightforward love story interwoven with much valuable historical information about one of the worst episodes of racism America has ever experienced. It would be an excellent movie for students in high school or college, or for ESL students. It could easily be used as a centerpiece for a social studies unit on this topic.

Suggested Usage

Previewing Activities

- Students could read *Farewell to Manzanar* by Jean Wakatsuki Houston. This true-life account of a young girl at Manzanar contains many scenes that students will see in the movie.

- Students could also watch the documentary *Guilty by Reason of Race* (NBC Films) about the internment of the Japanese.

- Students could locate Executive Order #2077, which started the internment relocation program. This is available as a government document in most major libraries and makes an excellent previewing activity.

Viewing Activities

Good Places to Stop and Talk

- For paired narration, use the scene in which the entire family is being shipped off to Manzanar.

 Bracknell and **Wokingham College**

- Students can be told to watch for Jack's evolving relationship with Papa Kawamura.

- Students can be told to watch / listen for other examples of discrimination toward Japanese-Americans. They will hear examples of laws regarding marriage and property ownership.

- Each member of Lilly's family represents a different Japanese-American approach to dealing with the internment and the issue of assimilation. Lilly marries a Caucasian and gets angry; Charlie elects repatriation to Japan; Harry elects to join the Nisei brigade and dies there; Papa Kawamura is suspected of cooperating with the FBI; Mama Kawamura seems to shrug it off with the attitude "Shikatagani." (It is fate. There is nothing to be done.) These attitudes are representative of many of the attitudes of Nisei. Students can be given a list of the attitudes and told to look for the character that best portrays each attitude.

Follow-up Activities

- Students can research to find out what eventually happened to the Nisei who were interned and what, if any, reparations they received.

- Students can research what eventually happened to the relatively few internees who elected repatriation to Japan in the middle of the war.

- Students can research the role the Nisei troops played in World War II.

- Local branches of the Japanese-American Citizen's League may have a speaker's bureau of persons who present talks on the internment issue. Teachers can invite such a speaker to discuss the issue with the class.

Other Considerations

There are a few sex scenes with some nudity. All the spoken Japanese is subtitled.

Ancillary Material

Guilty by Reason of Race. NBC Films, 1972.

Houston, Jeanne Wakatsuki, and James D. Houston. *Farewell to Manzanar*. Houghton Mifflin Company, 1973.

The Cotton Club

Subjects: 2, 3, 4, 7, 11, 20, 23
Playing Time: 121 minutes
Rating: R

Director: Francis Ford Coppola
Producer: Robert Evans
Date: 1984
Actors: Richard Gere, Gregory Hines, Diane Lane, Bob Hoskins, Fred Gwynne, Gwen Verdon, Nicholas Cage

Plot Summary

In 1928 Dixie Dwyer, a trumpet player, saves mob boss Dutch Schultz's life in a bombing assassination attempt. Dutch now "owes" Dixie and gives his younger brother a job. Meanwhile Dutch invites Dixie to a party, where he meets the owners of the famed Harlem, New York, Cotton Club—Owney Madden and Frenchy. Dutch asks Dixie to play piano for Vera, whom both Dutch and Dixie met the night of the bombing. Dutch has offered Vera her own club if she spends time with him, and even though Vera is interested in Dixie, she agrees to be Dutch's girl. Dutch also makes Dixie an offer he can't refuse—to work for him. The rest of the film concerns Dixie's attempt to get out from under Dutch's control and his encouraging Vera to leave Dutch. There are two subplots. One is the kidnapping of Frenchy; the other is about an African-American tap dancer, Sandman Williams, and his light-skinned girlfriend, Lila.

General Commentary

This is a very good drama to use as a resource in teaching any of the following subjects: America in the 1920s, the history of organized crime and violence in the United States, the history of entertainment in America, and racism. ESL students may find some of the accents difficult but should, nevertheless, be able to follow the basic story.

Suggested Usage

Previewing Activities

- Students might research and report on the causes and effects of Prohibition in the United States.
- Students might report and research on what life was like in the 1920s.
- Students can research and report on the Cotton Club and other clubs that existed in New York during the 1920s and 1930s.

Viewing Activities

GOOD PLACES TO STOP AND TALK

- Teachers might do a comprehension check after the scene in which, after Dixie saves Dutch's life, Dutch tells Dixie that he is his "Dutch uncle." This scene sets up the three major characters of the drama and establishes who Dutch Schultz is.

- Students might keep track of what Sandman and Lila experience, since it reveals the racism that existed at that time. It also reveals the limited options African-Americans had to "make it" in American society.

Follow-up Activities

- Students can write about or discuss what life was like for Sandman.

- Students can research and report on the lives of real performers who performed in New York clubs (such as Billie Holiday).

- Teachers might bring in more music from the 1920s and 1930s for students to listen to.

- Students can research Dutch Schultz and other famous American criminals of the early twentieth century.

- Students can trace the rise of different ethnic criminal organizations in America.

Other Considerations

None.

Ancillary Material

Haskins, Jim. *The Cotton Club*. New York: Random House, 1977.

Sann, Paul. *Kill the Dutchman! The Story of Dutch Schultz*. New Rochelle, New York: Arlington House, 1971.

The Court-Martial of Jackie Robinson

Subjects:	2, 3, 4, 7, 19, 23	**Director:**	Larry Peerce
Playing Time:	94 minutes	**Producers:**	Cleve Landsberg, Susan Weber-
Rating:	Mature		Gold, and Julie Anne Weitz
	(Parental Discretion)	**Date:**	1991
		Actors:	Andre Braugher, Daniel Stern,
			Ruby Dee

Plot Summary

Jackie Robinson is finishing up at the University of California at Los Angeles and making plans to get married. Before he can do either, he is drafted into the U.S. Army soon after the attack on Pearl Harbor. In the Army he attempts to get into officer's training school, but is thwarted by a racist officer. Eventually he becomes an officer with the help of boxer Joe Lewis. As an officer, he spends much of his time fighting racism in the military. He ends up being court-martialed for standing up for his rights. The movie ends with his acquittal and with his moving on to the next chapter / fight in his life—being the first African-American in major league baseball.

General Commentary

This is an excellent movie about the early life of a real man who fought racism in the military and in professional athletics. Many people don't know anything about this early part of Jackie Robinson's life. Teachers can use this film as a resource if they are teaching about racism or the African-American experience. ESL teachers should note that this movie is easy to listen to because all the main characters speak standard English and little or no idiomatic language is used.

Suggested Usage

Previewing Activities

- Students can research and report on segregation in the U.S. military.

- Students can study the Jim Crow laws. They are referred to in the movie

- Students might research and report on news accounts of Jackie Robinson's time in college and his time in the military.

Viewing Activities

GOOD PLACES TO STOP AND TALK

- The scene in which Jackie talks with another African-American soldier about wanting to become an officer is important because many other scenes depend on it. ESL teachers might want to do a comprehension check here.

- The scene in the cafe in which newspaper reporter Wendell Smith meets two baseball recruiters demonstrates the racism that kept African-Americans out of major league baseball. ESL teachers might want to do a comprehension check after this scene.

PATTERNS/STRUCTURES TO LOOK FOR

- Students can keep track by listing and describing the kinds of racism witnessed, felt, and experienced by characters in this film.

Follow-up Activities

- Students can research and report on Jackie Robinson's later life in baseball and the civil rights movement. Teachers might have students look at original sources (such as newspapers and magazines) for information.

- Students can write about Jackie Robinson's limitations in achieving the "American dream" and how he overcame them.

- Students might research the life of Joe Lewis, a supporting character in this story.

- Students can research the history of racism in professional baseball in America.

Other Considerations

None.

Ancillary Material

Robinson, Jackie (as told to Alfred Duckett). *I Never Had It Made*. New York: G.P. Putnam, 1972.

Dulfiume, Richard M. *Desegregation of the U.S. Armed Forces: Fighting on Two Fronts, 1939–1953*. Columbia: University of Missouri Press, 1969.

Crocodile Dundee

Subjects: 1, 4, 9, 25
Playing Time: 98 minutes
Rating: PG-13

Director: Peter Faiman
Producer: John Cornell
Date: 1986
Actors: Paul Hogan, Linda Kozlowski, John Meillon

Plot Summary

Mike Dundee is "Crocodile" Dundee, an Australian from the Outback whose reputation for wrestling crocodiles is worldwide. Reporter Sue Charlton goes to the Outback to write Croc's story. This comedy uses the fish-out-of-water story line. Charlton is out of place in the Outback, and Croc is out of place when he returns to New York City with Charlton. The two fall in love, but their romance is not what makes this film. What does make the film is the misunderstanding both characters have of each other's culture.

General Commentary

This film can be used in much the same way as *The Gods Must Be Crazy*. Students studying cultures may find this a comic view of culture. Teachers can also use this film as an example of a cross-cultural comparison. In addition, the film is filled with cliches and stereotypes that can be examined.

Suggested Usage

Previewing Activities

- Students can research and report on the Australian Outback.

- Students can brainstorm a list of stereotypes that are often used to describe Australians.

- Teachers may also want to bring in objects from other cultures and have the students list them and guess what the items are used for.

- Teachers may wish to have students research some of the features of Australian English.

Viewing Activities

GOOD PLACES TO STOP AND TALK

- The hotel scene in New York City is a good place to stop. Teachers may want students to refer to the third previewing activity above.

PATTERNS/STRUCTURES TO LOOK FOR

- Students may use their brainstormed list of stereotypes above and check off the ones that they find in the movie, and then add others that they notice in the movie.

Follow-up Activities

- Students can do a report on Australian slang and the meaning of the terms used in the movie.
- Student can do a comparative culture report on Australia and the United States.
- Students may consider the following questions and respond to them with regard to the movie:

    What is civilization?

    Is civilization necessarily progress?

- ESL students can report on what they found strange when they first came to the United States and what an American going to their country might find strange.

Other Considerations

None.

Ancillary Material

Wilkes, G.A. *A Dictionary of Australian Colloquialisms.* Sydney: Sydney University Press, in association with Oxford University Press, 1990.

Dead Poets Society

Subjects:	17, 10, 13	**Director:**	Peter Weir
Playing Time:	128 minutes	**Producers:**	Steven Haft, Paul Junger Witt, and Tony Thomas
Rating:	PG	**Date:**	1989
		Actors:	Robin Williams, Robert Sean Leonard

Plot Summary

In 1959 in a New England boys school called Welton Academy, the new English teacher encourages the boys to "seize the day." The boys decide to form a poetry society like the one their teacher formed when he was a student at the school. The movie focuses on the changes in several of the boys' lives. Neil, the main student character, is hounded by his father to go to medical school but discovers, through reading poetry, that he really wants to be an actor. He forges his father's signature on a permission slip after he wins a part in a community production of *A Midsummer's Night Dream*. His father, completely unconcerned about his son's feelings, forces Neil to withdraw from the play after one performance, and to leave his friends at Welton for a military academy. The night he is dragged away from the play, Neil returns to his parents' home. Feeling he has no control over his own life, he kills himself. The English teacher is blamed for Neil's suicide by the administration of the school because he encouraged the students to be free-thinkers. The teacher is forced to leave the school, but, as he leaves, his remaining students pay him an unusual and moving tribute.

General Commentary

This is a useful movie, although a bit melodramatic. It has as much to do with coming-of-age as it does with teaching styles and philosophies. It is recommended for secondary and ESL students, as well as for college students considering education as a career.

Suggestions for Usage

Previewing Activities

- Students might bring in a favorite poem and share it with the class.
- Students can write about or discuss their favorite learning experiences.
- ESL students can compare and contrast teaching styles in this country with those in their home country.

Viewing Activities

GOOD PLACES TO STOP AND TALK

- After the very first scene, ESL teachers might stop to make sure students understand the setting of the movie.

- The scene in which the boys bring their teacher's old yearbook and ask him about the *Dead Poets Society* is a good place for an ESL teacher to stop because it explains the whole premise for the formation of the society.

PATTERNS/ STRUCTURES TO LOOK FOR

- Students can keep a list of character-types of students in this movie. Todd is a younger brother living in his older successful brother's shadow; Cameron is a boy who likes a clear and strong authority figure; Knox is a romantic. A teacher might also have students write a short description of each and whether, and how, by the end of the movie each has or hasn't grown as a person.

Follow-up Activities

- Students might research the lives and poetry of some of the poets mentioned in this movie (such as Frost, Whitman, and Byron).

- Students can write poems or write about the importance of poetry.

- A teacher might want students to recite poetry.

Other Considerations

Teachers, especially secondary teachers, should note that the film contains a scene in which one of the main characters, a seventeen-year-old, commits suicide.

The Deerhunter

Subjects:	18, 19, 28	**Director:**	Michael Cimino
Playing Time:	183 minutes	**Producers:**	Barry Spikings, Michael Deely,
Rating:	R		Michael Cimino, and John Peverall
		Date:	1978
		Actors:	Robert De Niro, Christopher
			Walken, John Savage, Meryl Streep

Plot Summary

Three friends, Mike, Nick, and Steve, from the coal-mining regions of Pennsylvania go off to the Vietnam War with great expectations. While there, they are held captive by the Vietcong for a brief period. This becomes the turning point of their lives, as their captors force them to play Russian roulette against one another. Through Mike's careful plotting, they do escape, but not to anything better. Steve, newly married before going to Vietnam, loses his legs and ends up essentially abandoned in a VA hospital. Nick, engaged to Linda, loses his mind and runs away from the hospital in Saigon to become a strung-out Russian roulette player in the back alleys. Mike returns to Pennsylvania, where he eventually takes up with Linda. He returns to Vietnam, however, to fulfill his promise to Nick that he would not leave him there. There, in a roulette parlor, he challenges Nick to a game of roulette, and this time Nick gets the bullet instead of the blank. Mike brings Nick's body back to Pennsylvania for a decent burial.

General Commentary

This movie is bleak and oppressive, and doom seems to hang over it from the very first scenes. It is also a must-see if one wishes a comprehensive view of the impact of Vietnam on a generation of young men and their loved ones. One knows from the beginning, as the young men talk about taking out a deer with one shot, that they will be the deer and the shot will be what the rest of the movie is building toward. Nick's death at the end is a mercy killing, the destruction of a deer who wandered into the wrong part of the forest. This is an excellent film for mature high school, college, and ESL students.

Suggested Usage

Previewing Activities

• This movie should be presented in the context of a more focused study of the influence of the Vietnam War on Americans. As a minimum, students should know where Vietnam was, the years of the war, the numbers of Americans killed, and perhaps a little bit about the atrocities committed against prisoners of war. Very basic encyclopedia research should provide enough information about the war to frame the film, but it is definitely better if the film can be part of an extended study on the subject of Vietnam.

• Students may read and discuss excerpts from Mark Baker's book *Nam* as either a previewing or a follow-up activity, or both.

Viewing Activities

GOOD PLACES TO STOP AND TALK

- Depending on what a teacher is trying to teach, there are many excellent places to stop to talk about this film and to do comprehension checks. The scene in which Mike promises Nick that he will not leave him in Vietnam and the scene in which Mike and Nick discuss deer hunting and the importance of "one shot" are important. The scenes in which Steve explains to Mike about what has happened to him and the scene in which Mike returns home and avoids his welcome-back party are also important.

PATTERNS/STRUCTURES TO LOOK FOR

- This movie screams metaphor and symbolism. It is very important that students be advised to track the concept of "one shot" as it surfaces in the movie. Further, students should be encouraged to look at all scenes of deer hunting to try to figure out the meaning and symbolism of the movie's title. The scenes in which "one shot" are discussed—in Mike and Nick's home, in the Vietcong prison, and finally at the end as Mike and Nick play roulette—are all worth having students note. Students might be advised to try to figure out what the deer symbolizes.

Follow-up Activities

- The teacher will want to lead a discussion in which the significance of the idea of "one shot" and the deer are discussed.

- Students may contact their local office of the Veteran's Administration to find out about Vietnam veterans in the local area. Occasionally, it is possible to have a speaker from the V.A. address students on the Vietnam experience.

- Students can read and discuss excerpts from Mark Baker's *Nam: The Vietnam War in the Words of the Men and Women Who Fought There*, which provides oral histories of the era.

- Students can do local newspaper research to find out about local people who went to Vietnam and what happened to them.

Other Considerations

This is an incredibly tense and depressing movie. There are some scenes, for example of roulette, where the suspense is unbearable. The violence, both physical and psychological, is terrifying in places. There is one bedroom scene in which all the characters are clothed.

Ancillary Material

Baker, Mark. *Nam: the Vietnam War in the Words of the Men and Women Who Fought There*. New York: Morrow, 1981.

The Diary of Anne Frank

Subjects:	7, 10, 13, 14, 15, 17, 24, 31	**Director:**	George Stevens
		Producer:	George Stevens
Playing Time:	151 minutes (black & white)	**Date:**	1959
		Actors:	Millie Perkins, Diane Baker,
Rating:	None		Ed Jacobi, Joseph Schildkraut, Shelley Winters

Plot Summary

This is the true story of Anne Frank, a young Jewish girl, who goes into hiding from the Nazis at the age of 13 in Amsterdam during World War II. She is accompanied by her father, whom she loves; her mother, with whom she is often in conflict; and, her sister, Margot. The family is joined by Mr. Van Daan, a colleague of her father's; Mrs. Van Daan; and their son, Peter, whom Anne eventually falls in love with. They are soon joined by Mr. Dussel, a Jewish dentist. All hide in the attic of Mr. Frank's former business. They are assisted by two of Mr. Frank's former employees, Miep and Mr. Kraler. Eventually, they are discovered and taken to concentration camps, where only Mr. Frank survives.

General Commentary

This is a very important movie for students studying about the Holocaust, but don't overlook that at its core this is a coming-of-age story. The hitch is that as soon as the heroine comes of age, she is taken away to a concentration camp and dies. The movie does not explore what actually happened to Anne and her family in the concentration camp. This movie can be used with secondary, ESL, and college-level students.

Suggested Usage

Previewing Activities

• Students can read *Anne Frank: The Diary of a Young Girl* or excerpts from it. ESL teachers may wish to have students read *The Story of Anne Frank* by Eileen Prince, which is available through Heinle and Heinle publishers.

• Students might research and report on how Jews tried to escape from Europe before and during the implementation of Hitler's "final solution."

• Teachers might want to have students view a map of Europe and locate Amsterdam, Auschwitz (Oswiecim, Poland), and Bergen-Belsen (Germany).

Viewing Activities

GOOD PLACES TO STOP AND TALK

• For ESL students the second scene in the movie, beginning with the Franks' and Van Daans' arriving in the attic and ending with Mr. Frank telling everyone to go to their rooms, is a critical scene for understanding what their lives in the attic will be like. Mr. Frank tells everyone what they can and cannot do in the attic. ESL teachers can have students listen very carefully to this scene and write down the instructions that Mr. Frank gives the others.

- Teachers might want to stop right after the Hanukkah scene and right before the burglary scene. This is a good place for students to talk about what they have learned about Hanukkah. A lot of explicit and implicit information is given about Hanukkah traditions.
- The scene directly after the Hanukkah scene in which the burglar breaks in can be used by ESL teachers as the basis of a paired narration activity.
- Before or after any scene, students can act out its counterpart scene from the play *The Diary of Anne Frank*, dramatized by Frances Goodrich and Albert Hackett. This can promote comprehension, especially for ESL students.

PATTERNS/STRUCTURES TO LOOK FOR

- Students can keep a chart of Anne's interactions with all the characters in this movie, adding information about each as the movie progresses. This will help students see how Anne develops and changes as a person.
- Students can relate scenes in the movie (such as the bombing of Amsterdam, the news they hear on the radio) with actual historical events. It is interesting for students to find out how soon after Anne's death the liberation of Holland occurred.

Follow-up Activities

- Students can research what happened after Anne left the attic. A good resource for this is the book *Anne Frank, A Portrait in Courage*.
- Students can research what it was like to hide Jews. *Anne Frank Remembered* by Miep Gies is a book that describes what it was like to hide Anne and the others.
- Students can research Bergen-Belsen, the camp where Anne died.
- Teachers can invite a Holocaust survivor to speak to the students about his/her own experience.
- A number of documentaries on Anne Frank can be used as follow-up viewing.

Activities for Low-Level ESL Students

The following activities are suggested for use with low-level ESL students. A teacher can:

- have the students read a short biography of Anne Frank from an encyclopedia prior to watching the movie and tell each other what they have learned about her life.
- write a cloze passage of the first of Anne's diary entries and have the students listen for the missing words.
- assign different students to "be" different characters in the story. For example, one student could be Dr. Dussel, another Mrs. Frank, and still another Margot. Play the scene in which Mr. Van Daan is caught stealing food and have different characters write up the incident from their perspective. Have the students share their perspectives with the class.
- (prior to watching the Hannukah scene) have the students do encyclopedia research on the customs of this holiday. Then list the different gifts that Anne gives each person: a crossword puzzle book, a cigarette, ear plugs, etc., and have the students decide whom she will give each gift to, and why. Then watch the scene to see if they were right.
- play the burglary scene as a reported narration. Have half the students watch and report what they saw to the other half.
- use Anne's final diary entry as a cloze passage.

Other Considerations

This is a very depressing movie, and secondary students may need to talk about how they feel about the movie. The movie's few love scenes reflect Hollywood in the 1950s and may seem amusing to secondary students today.

Ancillary Material

Frank, Anne. *The Diary of a Young Girl.* Garden City, N.Y.: Doubleday, 1967.

Frank, Anne. *The Diary of a Young Girl.* Englewood Cliffs, N.J.: Globe Fearon Adapted Classics.

Goodrich, Frances, and Albert Hackett. *The Diary of Anne Frank* (dramatization). New York: Random House, 1956.

Gies, Miep, with Alison Leslie Gould. *Anne Frank Remembered: The Story of the Woman Who Helped to Hide the Frank Family.* New York: Simon and Schuster, 1987.

Prince, Eileen. *The Story of Anne Frank.* Boston: Heinle and Heinle.

Schnabel, Ernst. *The Footsteps of Anne Frank.* London: Pan Books, 1961.

Doctor Zhivago

Subjects:	14, 17, 25, 30	**Director:**	David Lean
Playing Time:	180 minutes	**Producer:**	Carlo Ponti
Rating:	PG	**Date:**	1965
		Actors:	Omar Shariff, Geraldine Chaplin, Julie Christie, Tom Courtenay, Rod Steiger, Alec Guinness

Plot Summary

This is the story of Yuri Zhivago, a Russian doctor and poet. Orphaned as a young child, Yuri comes to live with Tonya Gromeko and her parents. Yuri eventually becomes a doctor and marries Tonya. When World War I breaks out, Yuri is sent to the front to treat wounded soldiers, where he meets Lara, a nurse, who assists him. When he returns home to Tonya, he finds life in disarray. Moscow is a different place, and the Russian Revolution is about to explode. The family leaves Moscow for a small town in eastern Russia. There they attempt to lead a quiet life: Yuri writes poetry and Tonya tends the garden. One day in town, Yuri sees Lara whom he has not seen since the war. They immediately fall in love and an affair begins. Eventually the revolution reaches the countryside, and Yuri is separated from Tonya *and* Lara. Yuri finds his way back to his house to find Tonya and his family gone to France. Lara, on the other hand, is still there and welcomes him with open arms. But the revolution is still going on, and they are separated once again. After the revolution ends, Yuri settles in Moscow where, one day, he thinks he sees Lara as he is riding down the street. He dies of a heart attack before he can make contact with her.

General Commentary

This is an outstanding film, not only because of the story but because the cinematography is stunning and the score is haunting. This film can be used by language teachers whose students are reading the novel by Boris Pasternak or by teachers whose students are studying the Russian Revolution, world history, or love stories.

Suggested Usage

Previewing Activities

- Teachers may want to have students research Russian history from 1890 to 1921 to give them a better sense of the era.

- Students can create a historical time line to help them understand the movie better.

Viewing Activities

GOOD PLACES TO STOP AND TALK

- Teachers might stop at any scene where a major character is introduced in order to give students a better understanding of who people are and what is taking place.

- Teachers may have students identify characters as they reappear in the movie. This will help them grasp the movie better. It may even be necessary to keep a chart of the characters.

Follow-up Activities

- Teachers may want to assign the novel by Boris Pasternak and have students write a comparison / contrast paper reflecting upon the differences and similarities between the movie and novel. Teachers may have students explain how either the book, the movie, or both could have been perceived as being critical of communism.

- Teachers may also have students research other, more-recent communist revolutions or wars and write a paper on how people's lives were affected by the tragic events of the times.

- Secondary teachers might have students create a poster explaining the movie or attempting to sell the movie.

- Students can write an obituary of Yuri Zhivago.

- Students can read the poetry from the book by Pasternak.

- Teachers may have students do newspaper research to find out what happened to Pasternak when he was awarded the Nobel Prize for literature for this book.

Other Considerations

Although the movie is slow in places, it is an outstanding film. Its only drawback is its three hours and twenty minutes running time. Teachers may need to block time so it can be seen in its entirety in one or two days. It would be hard to understand if shown over a more-extended period of time.

Ancillary Material

Pasternak, Boris. *Dr. Zhivago*. New York: Pantheon, 1958.

Bolt, Robert. *Dr. Zhivago: The Screenplay Based on the Book by Boris Pasternak*. London: Collins and Harvill Press, 1958.

The Emerald Forest

		Director:	John Boorman
Subjects:	10, 12, 13, 21, 23, 31	**Producer:**	John Boorman
Playing Time:	113 minutes	**Date:**	1985
Rating:	R	**Actors:**	Powers Boothe, Meg Foster, Charley Boorman

Plot Summary

Tommi, the son of an American dam-builder in Brazil, is abducted by a band of Amazonian Indians called the Invisible People. His frantic parents are unable to find him. Ten years go by and the father once again sets off to search for his son, as he has been doing in his spare time for the last decade. After an incredible ordeal with a group of Indians called the Fierce People in which he is wounded, the father finds his son. He realizes that his son has a new life and returns to the city. Tommi is forced to venture into the city to locate his father after the women of his tribe are kidnapped and forced into prostitution. The father helps Tommi and the other men from the tribe to rescue the women and by doing so saves the tribe from immediate extinction. However, the father realizes that the dam he has been building will cause the ultimate extinction of his son's tribe. He goes to the dam to dynamite it, but before he can do so, the dam is destroyed by a flash flood, caused perhaps by the magic of his son's tribe.

General Commentary

On one level this drama can be viewed as a parable about what it means to be a responsible parent. The moral of the movie might be, being a good parent to your child means protecting the environment for your child. On another level this is a movie about Amazonian Indians and the destruction of the rainforest. This film can be used as a resource for any of the aforementioned subjects. It is recommended for all types of students; however, teachers should note that a great deal of this movie is in subtitles.

Suggested Usage

Previewing Activities

- Teachers might have students do a map exercise on the geography of Brazil with particular emphasis on the Amazon region.
- Teachers might have students research the lives and customs of some of the many Indian tribes along the Amazon.

Viewing Activities

GOOD PLACES TO STOP AND TALK

- ESL teachers can use any of the very good action scenes (such as when the father is being chased by the Fierce people) for paired narration activities.

Bracknell and Wokingham College

- Teachers might have students keep track of and describe the different customs of the Invisible People.
- Teachers might have students track the descriptive qualities of the names of the three different Indian tribes (the Bat people, the Fierce People, and the Invisible People).

Follow-up Activities

- Teachers might have students research and report on the destruction of the Amazon and its indigenous peoples, an issue that comes up often in the movie.
- Students might research and report on social problems in Brazil that are referred to in the movie (such as lost children and the urbanization of indigenous peoples).
- Students can do a creative writing assignment on what might happen to Tommi in the future or how an Invisible person might view the world outside the forest.
- After discussing what a parable is, students can do a writing assignment on how this movie might be called a parable.

Activities for Low-Level ESL Students

The following activities are suggested for use with low-level ESL students. A teacher can:

- play the scene in which Tommi is kidnapped and have the students write up a missing person's report as though they were Tommi's father.
- have the students watch the scene in which Tommi's father travels upriver with the Brazilian journalist. Script the dialog and have half the students listen for the Brazilian's comments and half listen for Tommi's father's responses. Ask the students comprehension questions about what they have learned about the rainforest from this conversation.
- play the scene in which Tommi's father and the Brazilian are captured by the Fierce people. Use this scene to do a paired narration.
- have the students write and perform a roleplay in which Tommi's father tells Tommi's mother about his meeting with their son. Have the students do this prior to watching the actual scene.
- (after watching the movie) have the students do impromptu oral reports in which they assume the roles of different characters and explain why the dam broke. The students can pull the following names from a hat: Tommi, Tommi's father, a worker at the dam.

Other Considerations

There is appropriate nudity among the Amazonian Indian characters.

Ancillary Material

Cowell, Adrian. *The Decade of Destruction: The Crusade to Save the Amazon Rain Forest.* New York: Henry Holt, 1990.

Mendes, Chico. *Fight for the Forest: Chico Mendes in His Own Words.* New York: Monthly Review Press, 1992.

Shoumatoff, Alex. *The World is Burning.* Boston: Little, Brown, 1990.

E. T.—The Extra-Terrestrial

Subjects: 1, 4, 26
Playing Time: 115 minutes
Rating: PG

Director: Steven Spielberg
Producers: Steven Spielberg and Kathleen Kennedy
Date: 1982
Actors: Henry Thomas, Dee Wallace, Peter Coyote, Drew Barrymore

Plot Summary

This fantasy film could have taken place in any suburb in America. In fact, it happened in Elliott's neighborhood and in Elliot's house. A visiting spaceship accidentally leaves one of its crew behind, and Elliott finds the being (E.T.) hiding in the shed behind his house. He befriends the creature and wants to keep him, but E.T. wants to "go home." While trying to help him get back home, Elliott and his brother and sister keep E.T. hidden from their mom and the federal agents who are trying to capture him. Eventually, Elliott is successful and helps E.T. get home.

General Commentary

Because this film was such a box office hit, many students will already have seen it. With that in mind, it is probably a good idea to approach it from a different point of view. Literature teachers may want to compare the apparition, E.T., to religious myth. ESL teachers may want to focus on the communication that goes on between E.T. and Elliott and why it is successful.

Suggested Usage

Previewing Activities

- Teachers may have students read reviews of *E.T.* prior to seeing the film. Students may list the things the reviewers liked and disliked about the film.
- Students can examine religious myths about visitations from the heavens prior to seeing the film.

Viewing Activities

GOOD PLACES TO STOP AND TALK

- There are many scenes in which E.T. and Elliott communicate. Students of ESL may want to note how they communicate and why they communicate effectively.

PATTERNS/STRUCTURES TO LOOK FOR

- Students can keep track of what makes E.T. so appealing. What qualities does he have, and what behaviors does he have that would make a human being be attracted to him?

Follow-up Activities

- Teachers may want to have students write a different ending to the story.

- Students can research religious apparition myths of other cultures.

- Teachers may have students roleplay situations in which they may only communicate with each other by means of gestures and mime.

- Students could gather information on UFOs and write a short story about a "close encounter."

Other Considerations

This movie has been seen by many people, so it is essential to try different approaches to teach the film.

Fahrenheit 451

Subjects:	15, 17, 18, 26	**Director:**	Francois Truffaut
Playing Time:	112 minutes	**Producer:**	Lewis Allen
Rating:	not available	**Date:**	1966
		Actors:	Julie Christy, Oskar Werner, Cyril Cusak, Anton Diffring

Plot Summary

Montag is a fireman of the future, but firemen of the future are not like firemen of today. They set fires instead of putting them out. The target of their fires is books, which no one may own or read. Montag's wife, Linda, has no problem with that; she sits "glued to the tube" for days at a time. Clarisse, the other woman in Montag's life, is a subversive teacher who secretly reads and keeps books. One day Montag steals a book he has been sent to incinerate. After reading it, he begins to collect books himself. Fearing for her life, Linda turns him in. Montag kills his captain and escapes with Clarisse to a forest where people commit books to memory. He begins to do the same.

General Commentary

This outstanding film looks at the importance of reading through the medium of film and is worth viewing again for those who have already seen it. English and social studies teachers can have a field day with all the social and literary questions this film poses. In addition, ESL teachers can use the film in conjunction with the novel of the same name. Anyone teaching about freedom of speech and the press and totalitarianism can use this film as a resource.

Suggested Usage

Previewing Activities

- Teachers can have students research historical and contemporary examples of book burning (such as in Nazi Germany, during the McCarthy era, etc.).
- Students can conduct experiments with burning paper and recording the temperature at which it burns.
- Teachers may have their students read the Bill of Rights and discuss the First Amendment.
- Students can read the book *Fahrenheit 451* by Ray Bradbury.

Viewing Activities

GOOD PLACES TO STOP AND TALK

- After any scene in which Linda is viewing the T.V. is a good place to stop. The teacher may ask the students to discuss how much time they spend in front of the T.V. and how much time they spend reading.

- Teachers may want to have the students record the book burning scenes, and discuss the attitude that exists while the burning is going on.

Follow-up Activities

- Students can compare and contrast the movie with the novel.

- Secondary teachers may have their students do a book drive and collect books from around their neighborhood for use in the school library.

- Secondary students can visit a fire station and research the job of a fireman today.

- Teachers may have students memorize poems of their choice.

- Teachers may ask students to watch less T.V. and read more books in a semester.

- Students can research and report on current book bannings around the country. A good resource for this information is the American Library Association (ALA).

- Teachers can have students answer the question: What book would you memorize and why? This activity is another way of having students write on their favorite book.

- Teachers may have students participate in National Banned-Book Week, which occurs in November.

- Students can research the life of Salman Rushdie, who was placed under an Iranian *fatwa* for writing *The Satanic Verses*.

Other Considerations

Some scenes may be inappropriate for younger students.

Ancillary Material

Bradbury, Ray. *Fahrenheit 451*. New York: Simon & Schuster, 1967.

Far and Away

Subjects: 1, 3, 25, 29
Playing Time: 140 minutes
Rating: PG-13

Director: Ron Howard
Producer: Brian Grazer
Date: 1992
Actors: Tom Cruise, Nicole Kidman, Colm Meaney

Plot Summary

The first part of this film is set in Ireland in 1892, where landowners are oppressing the peasants and only the rich can buy land. Joseph Donnelly, the son of a poor peasant, is shattered by his father's death at the hands of a bill collector working for a rich landowner. He sets off to avenge his father's death and finds the wealthy landowner, Mr. Christy. But before he can kill him, he is swept away by Christy's daughter, Shannon, who takes Joseph with her to America. They find themselves broke and trying to make ends meet where Americans don't like the Irish. Things don't look too promising for them. After a series of misfortunes the two are separated but are reunited in Oklahoma Territory in their search for land. And as in all good love stories, they get their land and each other as well.

General Commentary

This is an excellent film for teaching about American history or immigration. The two very popular actors do a good job of portraying their characters. Further, the film explores the following issues and themes: the political climate of the time, prejudice and ethnic tensions, and the idea of America as a "melting pot."

Suggested Usage

Previewing Activities

- Students can research and report on the reasons Irish immigrants came to the United States. A good source is *Real Lace: America's Irish Rich* by Stephen Birmingham.
- Students can research statistics on Irish immigration.
- Students can create a map showing the states where Irish immigrants settled and give the percentages of Irish in each area.

Viewing Activities

GOOD PLACES TO STOP AND TALK

- The scene in which Joseph Donnelly's father is dying may be a good place to stop. Mr. Donnelly says, "Land is a man's very own soul." The teacher may ask the students to respond to that statement.

- Students can look for the living patterns that the immigrants chose when they began to settle in America.
- Students can look for similarities in the economic status of people in Ireland and in the United States.

Follow-up Activities

- Teachers could have students research the political configuration of several large American cities in the 1890s and early 1900s.
- Students can examine political cartoons of the time to explore how politics and ethnic groups were treated.
- A research project on the land races in the western territories and states might interest some students.
- A research project on homesteading may prove interesting to some students.
- Students can research and report on the current wave of Irish immigrants, both legal and illegal, to the United States.
- Secondary students can research how their individual families came to the United States and report back to the class on their family immigration histories.

Other Considerations

Some students may find the brutal and bloody bare-knuckle boxing scenes unpleasant to watch.

Ancillary Material

Birmingham, Stephen. *Real Lace: America's Irish Rich.* New York: Harper & Row, 1973.

Potter, George W. *To the Golden Door; The Story of the Irish in Ireland and America.* Boston: Little, Brown, 1960.

Ferngully: The Last Rainforest

Subjects: 5, 9, 12, 20
Playing Time: 72 minutes
Rating: G

Director: Bill Kroyer
Producers: Ted Field and Robert W. Cort
Date: 1992
Voices of: Sheena Easton, Raffi, Christian Slater, Robin Williams

Plot Summary

This is the animated story of a tree fairy, Christa, and a human, Zak. Zak is busily employed cutting down the rainforest in which Christa lives. In the center of this rainforest is the evil tree-destroying force, Hexus, which has been entrapped in a twisted tree for as long as anyone can remember. One day Zak meets Christa, who promptly changes him into a wood sprite. Together they battle the force of Hexus, which has been let loose by the tree-cutting machine that Zak once worked on. It's a battle to save the rainforest, and it is won only when Hexus is finally entrapped again inside a tree.

General Commentary

There are some very adaptable elements in this movie, not the least of which is its use of metaphor and allegory. The tree machine "eats" trees. Hexus, the force which destroys, can be compared to the tree in the garden of Eden. The basic moral is simple: only that which is evil or stupid would dare to mess with the rainforest. The animation is clear, and Robin William's monologues as a bat-escapee from an experimental lab are equal to his best work in *Good Morning Vietnam* and *Aladdin*. The movie would work well with high school and young adults, as well as with ESL students.

Suggested Usage

Previewing Activities

- A teacher may have students study the question of rainforest deforestation prior to watching this movie.
- A teacher might preteach creation stories about how good and evil interact.

Viewing Activities

GOOD PLACES TO STOP AND TALK

- Numerous highly visual scenes can be used by ESL teachers for paired / mute / reported narrations. Some of these scenes include the scene in which Christa saves Zak from the tree-eating machine and the scene in which Christa battles Hexus in order to control it.

- The speech patterns of all the speakers are natural and filled with "speech fillers" such as "gee," "you know," and "well." ESL teachers may wish to have students focus on these features of natural speech.

Follow-up Activities

- Students could discuss the symbolism in the movie, including the symbolism of Hexus and the symbolism of Christa's battle with Hexus.

- A teacher may have students investigate and report on areas of the world threatened by deforestation and the reasons why these areas have been deforested.

Other Considerations

None.

Ancillary Material

Cowell, Adrian. *The Decade of Destruction: The Crusade to Save the Amazon Rain Forest.* New York: Henry Holt, 1990.

Mendes, Chico. *Fight for the Forest: Chico Mendes in His Own Words.* New York: Monthly Review Press, 1992.

Shoumatoff, Alex. *The World Is Burning.* Boston: Little, Brown, 1990.

Field of Dreams

Subjects: 7, 13, 17
Playing Time: 107 minutes
Rating: PG

Director: Phil Alden Robinson
Producers: Lawrence Gordon and Charles Gordon
Date: 1989
Actors: Kevin Costner, Amy Madigan, Gaby Hoffman, Ray Liotta, James Earl Jones, Burt Lancaster, Dwier Brown

Plot Summary

This sports fantasy film takes place in an Iowa cornfield. Ray Kinsella hears a voice in the field that says, "If you build it, he will come." With his wife's blessing, he tears up their cornfield and builds a baseball diamond. Sure enough, Shoeless Joe Jackson, or at least his ghost, shows up. (Shoeless Joe was Ray's father's hero.) Soon Ray sets out to bring others to this field of dreams. Although the bank wants to repossess his farm, he somehow makes things work. All the while, the family is treated to nightly baseball games played by ghosts from the past. Eventually the ghost of Ray's father appears, and Ray can finally make peace with him. Soon people from all over come to the field to see the games, and all turns out well.

General Commentary

This great fantasy film on America's favorite pastime, baseball, engrosses the viewer from the beginning. Even if you are not a baseball fan, you will probably like this movie. The film is based on the novel *Shoeless Joe* by W.P. Kinsella. Teachers may find this film of use while reading the book or studying the early years of baseball.

Suggested Usage

Previewing Activities

- The teacher may want the students to research and report on the origins and history of baseball.
- Students may be assigned to write short biographies of former baseball greats.
- Students can read *Shoeless Joe* by W.P. Kinsella.
- ESL teachers might teach students some basic baseball vocabulary.

Viewing Activities

GOOD PLACES TO STOP AND TALK

- Teachers may stop the film at the scene in which the community meeting wants to ban books. This would be a good place to talk about censorship and what place it has in the movie.

- Teachers may want ESL students to note the language used on the baseball field. Students can list the words and what they think their meanings are.
- Students can keep a list of the baseball players and what is special or different about each.

Follow-up Activities

- Teachers can ask students to respond to the question: Why are all the baseball players white?
- Students can research the Chicago Black Sox and the World Series of 1919.
- English teachers can have the students write an obituary for individual team members.
- Teachers may have students research the racial integration of baseball.
- ESL teachers might want students to write a dialogue between two ball players, using the language they listed under *Patterns/Structures to Look For*.
- Students can make an updated field-of-dreams team and give rationales for the selection of each team member.
- Students can research baseball today and then write about how baseball has changed since its inception.
- ESL teachers can take their students to an American baseball game for the cultural experience. ESL students can write about the game after they watch it.
- ESL teachers might have students read the poem "Casey at the Bat" by Ernest Lawrence Thayer.

Other Considerations

None.

Ancillary Material

Kinsella, W.P. *Shoeless Joe*. Boston: Houghton Mifflin, 1982.

Brown, Gene (ed.). *The New York Times Book of Baseball History: Major League Highlights from the Pages of the New York Times*. New York: Quadrangle / New York Times Book Co., 1975.

Gardner, Martin (ed.). *The Annotated Casey at the Bat: A Collection of Ballads about the Mighty Casey*. Chicago: University of Chicago Press, 1984.

Peterson, Harold. *The Man Who Invented Baseball*. New York: Scribner, 1973.

The Fisher King

Subject:	4	**Director:**	Terry Gilliam
Playing Time:	137 minutes	**Producers:**	Debra Hill and Lynda Obst
Rating:	R	**Date:**	1991
		Actors:	Robin Williams, Jeff Bridges, Mercedes Ruehl, Amanda Plummer, Michael Jeter

Plot Summary

Parry, a former history professor, is a homeless, mentally ill man who is kept on the streets by his quest for the Holy Grail. Jack Lucas is a depressed ex-disc jockey whose reason for living is a bottle of whiskey. The twist is that their lives are connected in an unusual way. Jack feels responsible for Parry's wife's death and the only way he can do penance is to help Parry. So Jack helps Parry find the Holy Grail (a silver trophy in a magazine). In the search Parry finds a friend, and when the search is over Jack finds forgiveness.

General Commentary

Although this is not a great movie, there are great moments. The scenes of the homeless in New York show a real image of the down and out. Likewise, the mental illness that plagues Parry can strike anyone—even a college professor. The scenes in the crowded subway have a magic about them that seems mystical. Teachers focusing on social problems may find this film helpful. Also, teachers of English may find this film useful as a resource for teaching fantasy.

Suggested Usage

Previewing Activities

- Teachers may have the students examine the issues surrounding homelessness (the causes, the effects, the demographics of homelessness, etc.).

- Students can research what "press accountability" means. Teachers can follow up by giving students ethical-dilemma questions.

- Teachers may have their students research the Holy Grail and its significance in history.

Viewing Activities

GOOD PLACES TO STOP AND TALK

- Teachers may want to stop the film when Parry is explaining to Jack why and how his wife died. Students can then discuss the responsibility of those who control the air waves.

- Teachers can stop the film when Parry is explaining his reasons for being homeless. Teachers may want to lead a discussion on mental illness and on other factors leading to homelessness.

- Students can look for and note the relationships Parry has with others as opposed to the relationships that Jack has with others.

Follow-up Activities

- Teachers may want students to visit a homeless shelter and/or a food bank.
- The teacher may invite a mental health expert to come to the class and share his or her knowledge of mental illness.
- Teachers might bring a local radio personality into the classroom for a discussion on responsibilities of the press.

Other Considerations

Some of the language may be offensive to some students.

Ancillary Material

Pyle, Howard. *The Story of the Grail and the Passing of Arthur.* New York: C. Scribner, 1933.

Gallipoli

Subjects:	14, 19, 30	**Director:**	Peter Weir
Playing Time:	111 minutes	**Producers:**	Robert Stigwood and Patricia Lovell
Rating:	PG	**Date:**	1981
		Actors:	Mel Gibson, Mark Lee

Plot Summary

This movie chronicles the lives of two young Australian men during World War I. Archy and Frank come from two totally different households, but both want the same thing—to get out. They meet at a national race and become friends. They see the prize money as a way to help them escape. Although their plan doesn't work out, they do find a way to escape: the army. When the two friends are reunited in training camp, they are excited to see the world. Their training camp in Cairo is a jumping-off place for British and Australian soldiers headed to fight the Turks. Both look forward to the war, but when they arrive at Gallipoli they realize it is more than they had bargained for. The conditions and poor leadership lead to a disaster, and both are killed.

General Commentary

This Australian antiwar movie looks deeper than just the horrors of war. It also explores the British prejudice toward the Australians and how senseless war really is. History teachers might find this film useful in discussing World War I, the cultural clashes between the British and Australians, British imperialism's effect on colonials, and the antiwar message that dominates the last part of the movie.

Suggested Usage

Previewing Activities

- Students can research the British, Australian, New Zealand, and Turkish involvement in World War I.
- Students can locate Gallipoli on the map and explain why controlling it might be important.
- Students can research and report on Australia's relationship with Britain.

Viewing Activities

GOOD PLACES TO STOP AND TALK

- Teachers can stop at the scene in Cairo prior to the men's departure for Gallipoli. The students can write down how the men feel at that time.
- Teachers might stop the film at the scenes in which the men are in Gallipoli and the fighting is in full swing to ask students the following questions: What are the feelings and attitudes of the men at this point? Compare them with the feelings of the men in the previous scenes. Why have they changed?

- Teachers might have students look for signs of discrimination and prejudice by the British toward the Australians.
- Teachers can have students note the different terms and slang used by the Australians and British and speculate as to their meanings.

Follow-up Activities

- Students can report on the events that led up to World War I.
- Students can watch other antiwar films and compare the messages.
- Students might write an imaginative dialogue between two characters using the British and Australian terms and slang they noted above.

Other Considerations

Some of the battle scenes may frighten some students.

Ancillary Material

Bush, Eric Wheler. *Gallipoli.* New York: St. Martin's Press, 1975.

Laffin, John. *Damn the Dardanelles! The Story of Gallipoli.* London: Osprey, 1980.

Liddle, Peter. *Men of Gallipoli: The Dardanelles and Gallipoli Experience.* London: Allen Lane, 1976.

Gandhi

Subjects:	7, 14, 15, 22, 23, 24	**Director:**	Richard Attenborough
Playing Time:	188 minutes	**Producer:**	Richard Attenborough
Rating:	PG	**Date:**	1982
		Actors:	Ben Kingsley, Edward Fox, Candice Bergen, Martin Sheen, John Gielgud, John Mills, Rohini Hattangady, Trevor Howard

Plot Summary

This epic biography of Mahatma Gandhi, the "Great Soul" of India, opens in South Africa, where Gandhi is a lawyer. Because of his color he is unable to accomplish much there, and he becomes a victim of the system. Later he returns to India to find that the British have made the people of his country second-class citizens. Gandhi vows to change the system and develops his ideas of civil disobedience—sometimes fasting for long periods of time—but always using non-violent tactics. The British do not like his methods or his philosophy, so they jail him. When he is released from jail for the third time toward the end of World War II, he becomes a major figure in negotiations for an independent India. In the end he is murdered by a Hindu fanatic who thinks Gandhi too tolerant of Muslims.

General Commentary

This film will be viewed for many generations. Not only does it tell the history of an incredible world leader, it also opens up a wealth of discussion on a variety of subjects. Teachers of any of the following subjects will find this film an excellent resource on culture, civil rights, human rights, imperialism, colonialism, India, South Africa, 20th-century world history, world leaders, and the non-violent civil disobedience movement.

Suggested Usage

Previewing Activities

- Teachers may assign students a research project exploring the history of India from the time before the British, operating as the East India Company, gained control of most of India.

- Teachers may divide the class into groups to report on the major religions of India: Islam, Hinduism, and Buddhism.

- Students can look up and define terms like *imperialism, colonialism,* and *the white man's burden.*

- Students can read some of Rudyard Kipling's poems such as "Gunga Din" and "The White Man's Burden" and afterward discuss what racism is.

- Students might study the history of imperialism in India.

- Students can do a map exercise that shows the different geographic and ethnic regions of India.

Viewing Activities

GOOD PLACES TO STOP AND TALK

- The movie has many scenes that are good places to stop. One at the beginning in which Gandhi is on a train in South Africa might be a good place to have students discuss his response to the situation.

PATTERNS/STRUCTURES TO LOOK FOR

- Teachers may have students note the patterns of Gandhi's response to the situations with which he is confronted throughout the movie.

Follow-up Activities

- Teachers may have students scan microfilm and microfiche of old newspapers to review the events that took place in India in the early and mid-1900s, including accounts of Gandhi's assassination. Teachers might direct students to old copies of *Life* magazine that might have used the pictures taken by the *Life* magazine photographer portrayed in the movie.

- Students may examine old obituaries of Gandhi from the microfilm and write their own.

- Students may also be encouraged to research others who have contributed to the non-violent civil disobedience movements who were influenced by Gandhi (such as Dr. Martin Luther King, Jr.).

- Students can study maps of how the British Empire has changed during the 20th century and write a summary of those changes.

- Students can research what motivated the British to establish an empire and what specifically was so appealing to the British about India.

- Students can research the effects of colonialism on India. For example, like many African countries, India was pieced together into a country from many different groups that are often in conflict with one another.

- Students can research Indian history from its independence until today.

- Students can study a country / colony of the British Empire currently seeking or in the process of receiving its independence (such as Northern Ireland and Hong Kong).

Other Considerations

The length of the movie is its only drawback.

Ancillary Material

Gandhi, Mahatma. *The Gandhi Reader; A Source Book of His Life and Writings*. New York: AMS Press, 1970.

Gold, Gerald. *Gandhi, a Pictorial Biography*. New York: Newmarket Press, 1983.

Rani, Asha. *Gandhian Non-Violence and India's Freedom Struggle*. Delhi: Shree Publishing House, 1981.

Shirer, William L. *Gandhi, A Memoir*. New York: Simon & Schuster, 1979.

The Gods Must Be Crazy

Subject:	9	**Director:**	Jamie Uys
Playing Time:	109 minutes	**Producer:**	Jamie Uys
Rating:	PG	**Date:**	1984
		Actors:	Nixau, Marius Weyers, Sandra Prinslo

Plot Summary

This comedy takes place in Botswana in South Africa and uses the Bushmen of the Kalahari to make many points. The film begins like a documentary and introduces a tribe of Bushmen who are uncivilized, non-violent, and non-materialistic. One day a small plane drops a Coke bottle on the tribe. The tribe believes it is a gift from the gods. As they begin to use the bottle, they find it can do many things for them. Soon everyone wants the bottle; they become violent and materialistic in the process. Realizing what is happening to them, they tell the tribe leader, Xi, to take the bottle to the edge of the earth and throw it off. Xi ventures to the "edge of the earth" and disposes of the bottle.

General Commentary

While some have called this film racist toward the Bushmen, it is still an excellent example of how people misunderstand cultures. This film provides a wealth of teaching material for many disciplines. Any teacher can use the film as an introduction to cross-cultural studies. ESL teachers have many opportunities to show how misunderstanding of some cultural artifacts can lead to miscommunication. Teachers can also use the film as the basis for many writing assignments.

Suggested Usage

Previewing Activities

- Teachers may bring in unfamiliar items from around the house. A Styrofoam faucet cover is an excellent choice. Local hardware stores carry them. Students take guesses about what the item is used for and then write an explanation of how it is used.

- Students may share experiences where they misunderstood what something was used for.

Viewing Activities

GOOD PLACES TO STOP AND TALK

- The many scenes that show the Bushmen using the bottle as a tool are good places to stop and ask students to suggest other uses for the bottle.

- Students can note all the different uses the Bushmen find for the bottle.
- Students may also be asked to note how the bottle changes the Bushmen from the beginning to the end of the story.

Follow-up Activities

- Teachers may ask students to bring something from home that is unique to their family or culture and explain its use after other students guess the purpose of the item.
- Teachers may pick a symbol from American culture and have students write an essay telling why the symbol is important.
- Students can look at some of Andy Warhol's more famous prints of cultural artifacts and write about why Warhol might have selected that particular subject.
- Students can design or write what they would include (and why) in a time capsule from their own culture and time.
- ESL students and students who have experienced another culture might write about or discuss a misunderstanding they had in or dealing with another culture.
- Students can research and report on the way certain cultures can affect the lives of indigenous peoples (such as the Amazonian Indians).
- Students can write what they think the moral of this story is.

Other Considerations

African students may take offense at how the Kalahari Bushmen are portrayed; this can be overcome by stressing the positive aspects of the movie.

Ancillary Material

Feldman, Frayda, and Jorg Schellman (eds.). *Andy Warhol Prints: A Catalogue Raisonné.* New York: R. Feldman Fine Arts, 1985.

Thomas, Elizabeth Marshall. *The Harmless People.* New York: Alfred A. Knopf, 1959.

Good Morning, Vietnam

Subjects:	7, 9, 18, 19, 28	**Director:**	Barry Levinson
Playing Time:	119 minutes	**Producers:**	Mark Johnson and Larry Brezner
Rating:	R	**Date:**	1988
		Actors:	Robin Williams, Forest Whitaker, Tung Thanh Tran, Chintara Sukapatana

Plot Summary

Adrian Cronauer is a disc jockey brought to Vietnam at the height of the war to raise the morale of the troops. He starts off each morning with the familiar cry "GOOOOOOD MORNING, VIETNAM." After that he attacks everything that moves. The top officers are annoyed by his behavior, but the troops love him. While he is there, he establishes a relationship with a young Vietnamese girl and attempts to teach her English. These scenes are not only funny but also very touching. He begins to mature while he is there; this is obvious in his jokes. At the beginning they are cheap and easy, but by the end of the film they are pointed and purposeful.

General Commentary

This is more than just a comedy. This film explores the war and the relationships that it created and destroyed, and it uses comedy as a vehicle to get the message across. The film is useful for classes studying the Vietnam War. For ESL students the humor may be difficult to understand in some places since much of it is based on cultural aspects; however, ESL teachers can use this film as a resource in teaching American humor.

Suggested Usage

Previewing Activities

- Students can research the Vietnam War.
- Students can research the role of famous wartime radio personalities, including propagandists Hanoi Hanna (Vietnam War) and Tokyo Rose (World War II).
- Teachers may bring in current "voices" from the armed service radio networks.

Viewing Activities

GOOD PLACES TO STOP AND TALK

- Teachers may find the scene in which Adrian confronts young soldiers who admire him, as they are just about to leave for the front a good place to have the students discuss the power of the media.

- Many of the monologues in this movie explore the metaphor of the movie *The Wizard of Oz*. As a previewing activity, the teacher may wish to have the students watch *The Wizard of Oz*. Following monologues in which Cronauer refers to the Ho Chi Minh Trail as the "Yellow Brick Road" and Hanoi Hanna as "The Wicked Witch of the North," the teacher may wish to stop the film and help students explore the comparisons that are made.
- Teachers may define "cynicism" and have the students pay attention to and note where and how cynicism is used by Adrian.

Follow-up Activities

- Teachers may ask the students if they think the film is antiwar, anti-military, or neither.
- Students can write a summary of the main character's time in Vietnam.
- Teachers could have a stand-up comic come to class and explain what it is like to perform as a stand-up comic.

Other Considerations

Other than the occasional use of offensive language, this film has no major drawbacks.

Ancillary Material

The Wizard of Oz. Directed by Victor Fleming. MGM / U.A. Home Video, 1939.

Gorillas in the Mist

Subjects: 7, 12, 17, 31
Playing Time: 129 minutes
Rating: PG-13

Director: Michael Apted
Producers: Arnold Glimcher and Terence Clegg
Date: 1988
Actors: Sigourney Weaver, Bryan Brown, John Omirah Miluwi

Plot Summary

This is the real-life story of Dian Fossey's African research on mountain gorillas. It examines her relationships with her married lover, *National Geographic* photographer Bob Campbell, students who come to study with her, her African tracker, the other Africans who work for her, the poachers and government officials that she goes up against, and the gorillas. The film traces her start in Africa, her setbacks, and finally her mysterious and unsolved murder.

General Commentary

This is an excellent film for high school, college, and ESL students who are studying endangered species and issues relating to that topic. Dian Fossey is portrayed as a dedicated but difficult person. The film is also visually breathtaking. Many American students may be surprised at the green and lush African scenery.

Suggested Usage

Previewing Activities

- Teachers might have students look up the writing and research Dian Fossey did for *National Geographic* as well as the article by Harold T.P. Hayes credited at the beginning of the movie. This could make an interesting library assignment.

- Students could do basic research on the mountain gorilla and on animal language studies (such as the Koko studies).

- Students might find out about anthropologist Richard Leakey and zoologist George Schaller, both of whom are quoted extensively in this film.

- Teachers can have students locate the countries Dian Fossey visits and works in on a map (the Congo and Rwanda).

- Teachers might have students study and research the political events in the Congo that are mentioned in the film.

Viewing Activities

GOOD PLACES TO STOP AND TALK

- ESL students might need time to understand the scene at the beginning of the movie in which Dian Fossey arrives in Africa, is met by Leakey, selects her trackers, and sets off for her camp. This scene is critical for setting up the movie's story.

- Teachers might have students view two scenes carefully. The first is when the *National Geographic* photographer points out that if it weren't for consumers outside Africa, gorillas would not be endangered. The second is when the Rwandan official tries to explain to her why he sold the baby gorilla to a zoo keeper. Both these scenes try to provide a balance to Dian Fossey's perspective.

PATTERNS/STRUCTURES TO LOOK FOR

- ESL teachers can use a number of scenes to teach language acts. Dian Fossey giving Bob Campbell orders with regard to how he should take pictures of the gorillas is an excellent scene for listening to imperatives. Dian confronting the zoo keeper in the restaurant is a good scene for listening to anger. The scene in the government official's office is a good scene for listening to bargaining.

Follow-up Activities

- Teachers can have students research the death of Dian Fossey by looking up accounts in newspapers and news magazines and finding her obituary. Students can then speculate about who might have killed her.

- Students can investigate and report on other endangered species.

- Teachers can have students write a critical response to how Africa and Africans are portrayed in this film. For an explanation of this point, see *Other Considerations*.

- Students could write a description of Dian Fossey's personality and how it changes during the film.

- Teachers can ask students to research why people poach and want to buy poached animals.

Activities for Low-Level ESL Students

The following activities are suggested for use with low-level ESL students. A teacher can:

- have students do a mute viewing of the first scene in the movie in which Dian Fossey is attending a lecture by Richard Leakey, up until Dian Fossey says to Dr. Leakey, "I'm Dian Fossey." Then turn on the sound. Teachers may want to preteach some vocabulary (*physical therapist, handicap, hell-of-a, to get close to, formal training, pre-veterinary, consideration, census,* and *to rough it*) and have students focus their listening by answering specific questions about Diane Fossey's and Richard Leakey's conversation, for example:

    Who is the woman?

    What does she request?

    Why does she think she is qualified to do what she is requesting to do?

    What rhetorical questions are used and for what purpose?

    Describe the woman's personality.

- stop the film and have students summarize the events of the story after Dian arrives in what was the Congo (now Zaire) until she gets to George Schaller's camp and is washing her face. Students should mention that she is met by Dr. Leakey at a small airport; other white people appear to be trying to leave the airport; Dr. Leakey takes her to a market where she meets some African men; one of the men is bold and talks to her; she picks the man to go with her; Dr. Leakey catches the plane that is leaving at the airport; Dian, the African man she picked from the group, and other African men leave in a jeep; Dian and her group leave the jeep and climb some mountains; Dian is helped by the African man she picked to come with her; they arrive at a place where there is a house; the Africans pitch tents and Dian washes her face. Even if no dialogue is understood from this portion of the film, the actions are understandable, and summarizing them will let students review the story up until this point.

- have students research and then discuss the causes of the civil unrest in the Congo. Students can then watch the scene in which Dian Fossey is forced out of the Congo and makes her way to a friend's house in Rwanda. Students can do a map exercise showing the Congo (Zaire), Rwanda, the border area, and the Virunga Mountains. This will help students understand the scene of her being forced out of the Congo as well as her later decision to study the gorillas on the Rwandan side of the mountains.

- have students do a mute viewing of the scene in which the African men confront Fossey in the mountains when she is with her tracker. Start where she sees the magic items hanging from the tree. Ask students to pay close attention to the body language the men display toward her, and then have students discuss what the men might think of Dian and how they know this. Students can then watch the scene with the sound and confirm or revise their assumptions. Again, this critical scene sets up the fact that, to many of the people living in the area, Dian was a witch, which she later used to give herself more power with the local people and which might have caused her death.

- have students look at some of Bob Campbell's photographs in *National Geographic*. Have students view the scene of Bob's arrival and do a focused listening / viewing for the following information:

   Who is the man?

   Why did he come?

   How does Dian treat him?

- ask students to narrate the scene that begins with Dian, her tracker, and the young female student looking at Digit and his group up until the time Dian kneels down before Digit's decapitated and mutilated body.

Other Considerations

If there is one flaw with this movie, it is that the African perspective is only briefly touched upon in the comments of Bob Campbell and the African official. Consequently, the motivations for the actions taken by the Africans are often glossed over. The only African who is portrayed sympathetically is Fossey's guide, who is seen as a helper, a subordinate. Further, the concerns of Africa's wildlife take precedence over the concerns of African people. Also students could be led to believe that it is white people who are the saviors of Africa. These issues / concerns need time for discussion, and students need to understand that they can be both appreciative and critical of this film.

Ancillary Material

Fossey, Dian. *Gorillas in the Mist.* Boston: Houghton Mifflin, 1983.

Leakey, Richard E. *One Life: An Autobiography.* London: M. Joseph, 1983.

The Graduate

Subjects:	10, 13, 17	**Director:**	Mike Nichols
Playing Time:	105 minutes	**Producer:**	Lawrence Turman
Rating:	PG	**Date:**	1967
		Actors:	Dustin Hoffman, Anne Bancroft, Katharine Ross

Plot Summary

This drama, set in 1967, is about a young man who returns home after graduating from college. He receives all kinds of advice about what he should do with his future. On the night of his parents' homecoming party for him, he is seduced by Mrs. Robinson—the calculating, bitter, alcoholic wife of his father's business partner. He ends up having an affair with her. As the affair continues his life becomes pointless, and he drifts aimlessly through his first summer after graduation. Then he meets Mrs. Robinson's daughter, Elaine. Pressured by his parents to date her, he invites her out and falls in love, something he wasn't prepared for and something he never felt for Mrs. Robinson. Mrs. Robinson threatens to tell her daughter about their affair, which has ended. So, to prevent Elaine from hearing it from her mother, Ben tells Elaine himself. Elaine is shocked and angered; she throws Ben out. After returning to college, Elaine agrees to marry a man she does not love only because it will please her parents. Ben hears of her quickly arranged wedding and desperately rushes to the church, just in time to see them saying their "I dos." He yells to Elaine and she looks at him, realizes that she loves him, and rushes for the exit of the church followed by her angry parents. Ben and Elaine put a crucifix in the door handles of the church to keep her parents and the mob of wedding guests from following them. Ben in tattered clothes and Elaine in her wedding dress jump on a passing bus. They have escaped!

General Commentary

For many, this movie represented the alienation many young people felt in the 1960s as well as the generation gap that existed between children and their parents. Anyone teaching about these issues or about the 1960s can use this movie as a resource.

Suggested Usage

Previewing Activities

- Teachers can have students read the novel by Charles Webb that this film was based on.

- Teachers might have students research what was happening in 1967 that might have contributed to Ben's sense of alienation.

- Teachers can have students discuss what alienation means and why people can feel alienated. Teachers might use the Simon and Garfunkle song "I Am a Rock" as a way of getting students to talk about the feelings people sometimes have when they are alienated.

Viewing Activities

GOOD PLACES TO STOP AND TALK

- The scene in which Ben's father's friend tells Ben he just has one word to tell Ben—"plastics"—is a good place to stop and have students discuss what they think the man and his advice represent.

PATTERNS/STRUCTURES TO LOOK FOR

- This movie is a character study of Ben. Students can keep a list of Ben's actions that demonstrate what kind of person he is. The scene in which Ben is in the hotel for the first time is wonderful for showing that Ben is a nervous, insecure, and guilty young man.
- This movie is also about how Ben changes. Students can keep track of the way and the reasons why Ben changes.
- The movie contains two very strong visual images of alienation. One is the scene in which Ben wears the wet suit and dives into his pool; the other is when Ben is drifting on the rubber raft in his parents' pool. Students can keep track of these images and discuss, after the movie, why they visualize alienation.

Follow-up Activities

- ESL teachers might want students to listen to and learn some of the songs from this movie, all now American rock-n-roll classics: "The Sound of Silence," "Scarborough Fair," and "Mrs. Robinson".
- Teachers might have students analyze the lyrics of "The Sound of Silence" to find images of alienation.
- This movie is also about a generation gap. Teachers can have students write how the two generations in this film differed from each other.
- The last thing that Mrs. Robinson says to her daughter in the church is, "It's too late." Elaine responds, "Not for me." Teachers might have students discuss what they think these words mean.
- Teachers might have students do a creative-writing assignment on what they think happens to Ben and Elaine.
- Students can compare and contrast the book and movie.
- Students can write or discuss if, how, and why they have felt alienated from their parents' generation.
- Teachers can discuss the possibility that Mrs. Robinson symbolizes the older generation sucking the life out of, controlling, and ultimately trying to destroy the younger generation, Ben. Students can write how Mrs. Robinson tried to do these things to Ben.

Other Considerations

The movie deals openly with adultery.

Ancillary Material

Webb, Charles Richard. *The Graduate*. New York: New American Library, 1963.

O'Brien, Geoffrey. *Dream Time: Chapters from the Sixties*. New York: Viking, 1988.

Guilty by Suspicion

Subjects:	3, 4, 8, 15, 22	**Director:**	Irwin Winkler
Playing Time:	105 minutes	**Producer:**	Arnon Milchan
Rating:	PG-13	**Date:**	1991
		Actors:	Robert De Niro, Annette Bening, George Wendt

Plot Summary

This drama about David Merrill, a Hollywood director, begins as he returns from a couple of months in Europe. He discovers that the husband of a good friend has not only testified to the House Committee on Un-American Activities that he and others had communist ties, he has also testified against his own wife, who commits suicide. Darryl Zanuck, the studio head for whom David has been working, tells David that before he can continue working on the film he is making, he must clear things up with the House Committee on Un-American Activities. Merrill refuses and soon finds himself blacklisted. He loses his house, his job, his ability to get work, and many of his friends and professional contacts. Finally, he is forced to testify in front of the House committee. He refuses to inform on others and finds himself in contempt of Congress. He leaves the congressional court room having won a victory with no tangible spoils.

General Commentary

Anyone teaching about the effects of the Cold War, McCarthyism, or ethics will find that this is a very good movie to use. It is appropriate for any type of student. ESL students and some American students might really be surprised at this period of American history. The story is a graphic example of the effects of McCarthyism on individual Americans.

Suggested Usage

Previewing Activities

- Teachers might have students research and report on Joseph McCarthy and what the House Committee on Un-American Activities was, since this is critical to understanding the movie.

- Students can also research and report on the causes and effects of the Cold War (atomic weapons, the Korean War, and the Ethel and Julius Rosenberg affair). Each of these examples are referred to in the movie.

- Students can find out who Darryl Zanuck was. He is one of the many characters in this movie.

- This movie refers to the Constitution on a number of occasions. Characters in the movie talk about things being unconstitutional and "taking the Fifth." Teachers might have students look at what the Constitution says about freedom of speech and the right not to incriminate oneself.

Viewing

- ESL teachers might want to do a comprehension check after the scene in the hotel room in which David Merrill talks to his lawyer and a government official, since it presents the dilemma that David is in.

PATTERNS/STRUCTURES TO LOOK FOR

- The effects of McCarthyism and blacklisting are examined throughout the film; therefore, teachers might have students keep track of all the ways people's lives were affected (such as losing one's home, child, job, ability to keep employment, friends, and life).

Follow-up Activities

- Teachers might want students to research and report on why some people in America did become interested in communism in the 1930s.

- Students can research which Hollywood actors were affected by McCarthyism. Students can research those that informed on others, those that were informed on, and those who refused to inform.

- Students can also research other types of Americans who were affected by McCarthyism (intellectuals, scientists, politicians).

- A scene in the movie involves book burning. Teachers might have students research what books are banned in different parts of the United States today.

- Teachers might want students to write or discuss what they might have done if they had been put in David Merrill's position or what they think being a good American means.

- Students can find, describe, and give their opinions about other, past or present, attempts to force people to take loyalty oaths.

Other Considerations

None.

Ancillary Material

Belfrage, Cedric. *The American Inquisition.* Indianapolis: Bobbs Merrill, 1973.

Griffith, Robert. *The Politics of Fear: Joseph R. McCarthy and the Senate.* Lexington: University Press of Kentucky, 1970.

Gung Ho

Subjects:	4, 6, 9, 23	**Director:**	Ron Howard
Playing Time:	111 minutes	**Producers:**	Tony Ganz and Deborah Blum
Rating:	PG-13	**Date:**	1986
		Actors:	Michael Keaton, Gedde Watanabe, George Wendt, Mimi Rogers

Plot Summary

An American auto worker is sent to Japan to ask a Japanese auto company to reopen a closed American car factory in his small midwestern industrial town. He is successful, and the Japanese arrive in town and reopen the factory, but in the process many changes occur. The changes mostly revolve around cultural differences between Japanese and American work styles and lifestyles. The film ends predictably with both the American main character and Japanese main character changing in order to achieve a goal that both want.

General Commentary

Because this movie employs many stereotypes of Japanese and American blue collar workers, it can be used as a tool for American students to explore their own stereotypes of Japanese. It can also be used with ESL students as a way to examine stereotypes and cross-cultural differences. This movie would be useful for secondary and ESL students dealing with the above-mentioned subjects.

Suggested Usage

Previewing Activities

• Students might think about and write down their images and stereotypes about the Japanese.

• ESL students might write down or discuss life style and work style differences between Americans and people in their own country.

Viewing Activities

GOOD PLACES TO STOP AND TALK

• For students to examine all the stereotypes / images presented in this film, a teacher might stop the film every half hour to let students discuss with each other and list what they have observed about the Japanese and Americans in the film. A teacher might keep a list or chart of the stereotypes and images.

• A teacher can clip any of the many scenes from this movie that demonstrate the communication problems between the Americans and Japanese and have students listen for why these problems occur.

- Students can list or keep a chart of the different types of Japanese and the different types of Americans they observe in the movie.

Follow-up Activities

- Students can do readings on contemporary Japanese life and compare what they learn from the readings to what was presented in the film.

- Students can interview a Japanese person who is living or visiting the United States about his/her thoughts on the stereotypes and images presented in the film.

- Students can watch other films that deal with the larger issue of stereotypes many Americans have, and have had, about Asians and Asian-Americans. A recommended documentary on this subject is the short film *Misunderstanding China*, which deals well with the stereotypes Hollywood and American society had/has of Chinese Americans.

Other Considerations

This film has no drawbacks if a teacher uses it as a means of examining stereotypes. But if it is presented as a realistic dramatization, some students might be offended by it.

Ancillary Material

de Mente, Boye. *How to Do Business with the Japanese: A Complete Guide to Japanese Customs and Business Practices.* Lincolnwood, IL: NTC Business Books, 1987.

Misunderstanding China. CBS News, 1972.

Hamlet

Subjects:	13, 17	**Director:**	Franco Zeffirelli
Playing Time:	135 minutes	**Producer:**	Dyson Lovell
Rating:	PG	**Date:**	1990
		Actors:	Mel Gibson, Glenn Close

Plot Summary

This movie follows Shakespeare's basic plot. Hamlet, the prince of Denmark, broods that his mother has waited a mere two months to marry his uncle, Claudius, following the untimely death of his father. One dark night, he meets the ghost of his father, who tells him that indeed his uncle had murdered his father. Seriously disturbed, Hamlet determines to expose his uncle. He has a passing band of troubadours reenact the crime, but his uncle does not break down. Hamlet's brooding obsession results in the madness and suicide of his love, Ophelia, but still Hamlet does not refrain from his intent to expose his uncle. At a tournament, his uncle sets about to kill Hamlet and manages to kill his wife, Gertrude, accidentally. Hamlet is killed at the same tournament, as is Claudius.

General Commentary

Although lavishly filmed and reasonably well acted, this movie is not for the novice Shakespeare viewer. The lines are spoken in English that approximates the original version grammatically and lexically, but the accents are American. In addition, of all Shakespeare's plays, this is one of the more complex plots. There are two schools of thought on how best to proceed with such a film: allow the students to view it and then teach it, or teach it and then allow the students to view it. In the interest of keeping student interest from flagging on the subject of Shakespeare in general and this play in particular, it is best to preteach as much as possible. With good preteaching, the film is appropriate for all levels from high school through college and ESL.

Suggested Usage

Previewing Activities

- The students can read a summary of the play, such as that by Charles and Mary Lamb in *Favorite Tales from Shakespeare*.

- The teacher can provide students with some of the more famous "lines" from *Hamlet* and ask the students to say what they think the lines mean. These are some of the more famous lines from this play:

    "To be or not to be, that is the question."

    "The play's the thing."

    "Frailty, thy name is woman."

    "Get thee to a nunnery."

    "To thine own self be true."

- The teacher can preteach some of the more common Shakespearean English utterances in the play, including *thee*, *thy*, *thou*, and *faith*.
- The students can read and perform the actual play or parts of it. ESL teachers and teachers of high school students may wish to use a modernized written-down version of the play.

Viewing Activities

GOOD PLACES TO STOP AND TALK

- Teachers might find it useful to stop and talk at the end of each major scene. At the very least, they would be well advised to stop and check for comprehension at the following junctures:

    after Hamlet's opening, when it is firmly established that Hamlet is bemoaning the death of his father and the upcoming marriage of his mother

    after the scene in which Hamlet speaks with the ghost of his father

    after the scene in which Hamlet decides to approach the troubadours

    after the scene in which Hamlet repudiates Ophelia

PATTERNS/STRUCTURES TO LOOK FOR

- If the teacher has pretaught lines from the play, students can listen for those lines and note the meaning they are given in the play itself.

Follow-up Activities

- Students could read and perform a particular scene that they enjoyed from the play.
- Since Shakespeare's themes are often borrowed by writers from many different countries, students can be encouraged to think of other examples of the same story that they may have read or seen enacted. This can be done either orally or in writing.
- Students can explore the history of the relationship between Denmark and England, which is only alluded to in this play.
- Where possible, students can view the play and compare the play and the movie.

Other Considerations

The complexity of the language and plot is the only possible problem posed by this movie. If the play is pretaught, this should not represent a problem to students, either ESL or those for whom English is a first language.

Ancillary Material

Shakespeare, William. *Hamlet*. Ed. Harold Bloom . New York: Chelsea House, 1990.

Shakespeare, William. *Hamlet*. Globe Masterworks.

Lamb, Charles, and Mary Lamb. *Favorite Tales from Shakespeare*. New York: Grosset & Dunlap, 1956.

High Road to China

Subjects: 1, 9, 25, 31
Playing Time: 105 minutes
Rating: PG

Director: Brian G. Hutton
Producer: Raymond Chow
Date: 1983
Actors: Tom Selleck, Bess Armstrong

Plot Summary

This adventure film is set during the Roaring Twenties. Eve Tosser is an heiress who must find her missing father to secure her rights to his company. She hires Patrick O'Malley, a World War I flying ace, to help her in her search as she flies across Central Asia on a trip that starts in Istanbul and ends in Sinkiang, China. The film depicts their various adventures with the British, the restless natives of Afghanistan, the Nepalese Buddhists, and the Chinese peasantry.

General Commentary

This is definitely a pleasing film to watch. The scenery is magnificent, the aerial stunts and photography are unbelievable, the spirit of the Jazz Age is well captured, and the deft comedy is well written. This is a film that could be used with a secondary or ESL audience to stimulate a further quest for knowledge about certain subjects.

Suggested Usage

Previewing Activities

- The students could research the history of military aviation, with particular emphasis on the battle of Verdun in World War I.
- The students might look at a map of the world in the 1920s to find the countries (Turkey, Afghanistan, Nepal, China) that are flown over in this film.

Viewing Activities

Good Places to Stop to Talk

- Teachers of ESL students may wish to use the opening scene or any of the many aerial stunt scenes to do paired narrations.

Patterns/ Structures to Look For

- There are several excellent scenes in which the two main characters disagree. ESL students could listen for and write down some of the ways in which the two main characters express disagreement.
- There are also excellent scenes in which the two main characters are actively requesting information about Eve's father. ESL students could note the language used to request information.

Follow Up Activities

- Teachers might have students compare / contrast a map of the world in the 1920s with a current map of the world.
- ESL teachers might have students roleplay scenes of disagreement or information-requesting.
- Students could answer questions about what they learned about each of the cultures shown in the film: British colonial, Afghani native, Nepalese Buddhists, and pre-Communist Chinese peasants. They could then be sent to an encyclopedia to verify the accuracy of what they have learned.

Activities for Low-Level ESL Students

The following activities are suggested for use with low-level ESL students. A teacher can:

- make a cloze passage of the scene in which Eve and Charley discuss why she must find her father. Emphasize content words. This scene establishes the reason for the trip.
- have students listen in pairs for the different halves of the dialog in which Eve and O'Malley negotiate the price of the trip to China. One student can listen for Eve's lines, the other for O'Malley's responses.
- play the scene mute in which Eve is talking to the British soldier after dinner and then goes to fight with O'Malley. Then have the students write the dialog they think is being spoken.
- play the scene in which O'Malley drops a Afghani native out of his plane as a paired narration.
- rehearse information questions and then play the scene in which O'Malley and his mechanic ask the Buddhist monk for information about Eve's father. Do this as a modified info-gap activity, with some of the students having the questions and listening for the answers and other students having the answers and listening for the questions.
- play the movie from the time Eve and O'Malley land in China until just before her father appears. Play it once and ask students to predict what will happen to Eve and O'Malley.

Other Considerations

ESL teachers should note that although the two main characters speak straight American English, a variety of other characters speak either in dialect or with accents. None of these, however, should affect comprehension of this very visual film. Also, one episode with a tribe of warlike Afghani natives might be offensive to students from that country.

Hoffa

Subjects:	4, 7, 11, 22		**Director:**	Danny DeVito
Playing Time:	140 minutes		**Producer:**	Edward R. Pressman
Rating:	R		**Date:**	1992
			Actors:	Jack Nicholson, Danny DeVito

Plot Summary

Told in flashbacks, this film documents the life of Jimmy Hoffa, president of the International Teamsters. The film continually returns to a gas station where Hoffa is waiting for someone. The first flashback is to the 1930s with Hoffa trying to rally interest in the local unions in the Midwest. It continues as Hoffa begins to grab power wherever he can. Soon Hoffa is making contacts with whomever (including organized crime) will help him get and keep that power. It documents his arrest and conviction for misuse of union pension funds, and his feud with Bobby Kennedy. The final flashback reveals that Hoffa has been set up, and he is killed as he sits in his car. The mystery of where Hoffa is buried has never been answered.

General Commentary

This movie does a thorough job of examining the life and times of Jimmy Hoffa. Jack Nicholson does a fantastic job of acting and actually looks very similar to Hoffa. Anyone teaching about the American labor movement and the connection between labor, organized crime, and the government will find this film a good resource.

Suggested Usage

Previewing Activities

- Teachers may have students research the beginnings of the labor movement in the United States.

- Teachers may have students create a list of unions that are found in the community.

- Students may interview union leaders and corporate managers to see what both sides think of unions.

- Students may research and report on organized crime and its dealings with the labor movement.

Viewing Activities

GOOD PLACES TO STOP AND TALK

- Teachers may want to stop the film at the scene in which Hoffa first becomes involved with organized crime and ask the students whether they see Hoffa as a labor idealist or an opportunist.

- Teachers may want the students to note the violence that was a constant threat whenever the union wanted more concessions.

Follow-up Activities

- Students might research and write a brief biography or obituary of Jimmy Hoffa.
- Students might examine old newspaper articles on Hoffa and the teamsters and relate them to scenes in the movie.
- The class might debate the usefulness of unions in present-day economics.
- The teacher may bring in guest speakers from unions and from management and have them discuss the NAFTA Treaty and the GATT Treaty.

Other Considerations

Some students might find the language and nudity objectionable.

Ancillary Material

Sloane, Arthur A. *Hoffa*. Cambridge: MIT Press, 1991.

Home Alone

Subjects:	9, 13, 17		**Director:**	Chris Columbus
Playing Time:	102 minutes		**Producer:**	John Hughes
Rating:	PG		**Date:**	1990
			Actors:	Macaulay Culkin, Joe Pesci, Catherine O'Hara, Daniel Stern

Plot Summary

A little boy, Kevin McCallister, is accidentally left home alone when his family leaves on a vacation. The movie depicts what Kevin does to protect his house from two very determined burglars. Several minor plots detail his mother's attempt to get back from Paris to Chicago, and Kevin's discovery that his next-door neighbor is not the crazy mass-murderer that his older brother had convinced him he was. In the two days that Kevin is home alone, he realizes that he really does love his family. The criminals are caught after suffering from Kevin's cartoon-like defense of his house, and Kevin is reunited with his family.

General Commentary

This very funny movie can be used to teach a number of structures to ESL students. It can also be used as a supplement to teaching the O. Henry short story *Ransom of Red Chief* because both stories turn the victim into the victimizer. In addition, it can be used to teach students how to become more critical viewers of movies. It is recommended for ESL and secondary students.

Suggested Usage

Previewing Activities

- Students can read the O. Henry short story *Ransom of Red Chief.*

- Teachers can have students view any violent cartoon such as the "Road Runner" and note what kind of violence is portrayed.

- ESL students, depending on their level, can review cause-and-effect transitions, such as *because*-clauses or conditionals, to prepare for the first *Patterns/Structures to Look For* activity below.

Viewing Activities

Good Places to Stop and Talk

- It is important that ESL students understand what Kevin's older brother is saying about their next-door neighbor, because the scene explains why Kevin is so scared of the elderly man. ESL teachers might have their students view this scene very carefully.

- In the beginning of the movie, three critical events lead to Kevin being left at home: Kevin causes the milk to be spilled on the pizza, a tree falls on a power line, and a neighbor boy shows up at the house. ESL students, depending on their level, can practice retelling the events that lead to Kevin being left at home. *Because*-clauses and conditionals can be useful in doing this.

- The scenes in which the burglars attack the house are full of cartoon-like violence. The burglars survive all kinds of punishment that would ordinarily kill or maim them seriously. Students who are already aware of what kinds of violence is seen in cartoons can list and describe the kinds of cartoon-like violence. This is a useful activity for getting students to become more critical viewers of movies.

Follow-up Activities

- Students can be asked to compare the two young boy characters in the movie and in the O. Henry short story.

- Students can write a critical review of the violence in the movie.

- Students can write about what Kevin learns about himself and others during this movie.

Other Considerations

Dennis the Menace, a movie released in the summer of 1993, is a good follow-up movie on the subject of victim becoming victimizer.

Ancillary Material

Henry, O. Memorial Committee. *Great American Short Stories: O. Henry Memorial Prize-Winning Stories 1919–1934*. Garden City, N.Y.: Doubleday, 1934.

The House on Carroll Street

Subjects: 3, 8, 22
Playing Time: 100 minutes
Rating: PG

Director: Peter Yates
Producers: Robert F. Colesberry and Peter Yates
Date: 1988
Actors: Kelley McGillis, Jessica Tandy

Plot Summary

Emily Crane, a college-educated career woman, loses her job as a photo editor for *Life* magazine because she refuses to turn over to a McCarthyesque congressional committee subpoenaed documents of a leftist organization to which she belonged. Still under surveillance by the FBI, she goes to work as a reader for a near-blind elderly lady. Seated in her employer's backyard, she overhears the congressional aide who tormented her conversing with a German man in the house on Carroll Street, next to her employer's home. Intrigued, she befriends the young boy whom she saw acting as a translator for the congressional aide. When he takes up her offer of friendship and assistance, he is stabbed to death in her arms, and she is left to unravel the mystery of the house on Carroll Street. Who was the German man? Why was he shouting? What business did he have with this congressional aide? As she searches for the answers to these questions with the help of Cochran, her FBI surveillant who has fallen in love with her, she discovers that the German is an escaped Nazi doctor who is being protected by the congressman in the interest of national security. The denouement occurs when the congressional aide falls to the death he deserves and the FBI agent saves the day by arresting the Nazi and his friends.

General Commentary

This movie has all the features of a political thriller: it's set in a recognizable period—the McCarthy era; it has a romance; the government is the heavy throughout; and good citizen Crane is responsible for the FBI developing a conscience. Escaped Nazis and evil congressional aides make wonderful bad guys. It is exciting and even believable, but definitely complex. The movie has a lot to offer a class if it's properly pretaught and if it's restricted to a late high school, college, or very advanced ESL audience.

Suggested Usage

Previewing Activities

- The teacher could prepare the students by teaching the history of the McCarthy hearings on "un-American" activities. Students may find it interesting to investigate newspaper clippings from the time of the hearings, particularly clippings about individuals who refused to cooperate with the hearings. ESL students, particularly those from the former Soviet Union and the People's Republic of China, often find it amusing to learn that the hearings were essentially a reaction to the "red menace" of their countries.

- If the film is going to be shown to ESL students, the teacher could have students do an encyclopedia project to learn about the jurisdictions of the FBI and the Justice Department.
- The film deals with the issue of Nazis seeking refuge in America. Prior to watching, teachers may wish to have students do research, through newspaper indexes, on Nazis who have been found in America. Mention is made of Nazis being allowed into America to assist with the rocket program.
- Teachers may wish to review basic legal terms and concepts, including *subpoena*, *in contempt*, *search warrant*, and *civil liberties*. At a minimum, student should be familiar with the basic liberties guaranteed in the Bill of Rights.

Viewing Activities

GOOD PLACES TO STOP AND TALK

- For basic comprehension checks, the teacher should stop the tape and discuss the film after the scene in which Emily refuses to surrender documents to the committee, and all scenes in which Emily talks to the congressional aide.

PATTERNS/STRUCTURES TO LOOK FOR

- In many scenes Emily must confront people, particularly the congressional aide, who are attempting to deny her her basic rights. In these scenes she conveys hostility, anger, and unwillingness to cooperate. ESL students can be directed to look for these scenes and to make note of the language and body language that Emily uses to make her point. Of particular note is her use of silence, which ESL students often misinterpret as fear.

Follow-up Activities

- The teacher can lead a discussion focused on what the students have learned about the McCarthy era and the Nazis in America.
- Any of the previewing activities can be extended. Students may find it particularly interesting to find out more about people who served with McCarthy in the hearings, particularly Roy Cohn and Robert Kennedy. Teachers may wish to assign students to do biographies of some of the more famous individuals who served on the hearings.
- The teacher may have students investigate the liberties guaranteed in the Bill of Rights and investigate important contemporary issues based on issues raised by the Bill of Rights.
- The teacher may have students do follow-up research to find out what happened to some real-life people who refused to give the McCarthy hearings the information they sought. Of particular interest is the story of the Hollywood Ten and, in particular, the story of Ring Lardner Jr., who triumphed over the hearings and eventually won an Academy Award for *M*A*S*H*. Students in the class could be assigned to research the lives of different members of the Hollywood Ten.

Other Considerations

There are one brief moment of upper-body female nudity and one scene in which sex is alluded to.

Ancillary Material

Belfrage, Cedric. *The American Inquisition.* Indianapolis: Bobbs Merrill, 1973.

Blun, Howard. *Wanted! The Search for Nazis in America.* New York: Quadrangle / New York Times Book Co., 1977.

Dick, Bernard. *Radical Innocence: A Critical Study of the Hollywood Ten.* Lexington: University of Kentucky, 1989.

Griffith, Robert. *The Politics of Fear: Joseph R. McCarthy and the Senate.* Lexington: University Press of Kentucky, 1970.

Kahn, Gordon. *Hollywood on Trial: The Story of the Ten Who were Indicted.* New York: Boni and Gaer, 1948.

Inherit the Wind

Subjects:	3, 4, 7, 24	**Director:**	Stanley Kramer
Playing Time:	128 minutes (black & white)	**Producer:**	Stanley Kramer
		Date:	1960
Rating:	G	**Actors:**	Spencer Tracy, Fredric March, Gene Kelly, Dick York

Plot Summary

Based on the Scopes trial of 1925, this drama centers around the trial of a public school teacher, Burt Cates (who is supposed to be John Thomas Scopes), who has been arrested for teaching evolution. He is defended by Henry Druham (who is supposed to be Clarence Darrow) and is prosecuted by Matthew Harrison Bradey (who is supposed to be William Jennings Bryan). In the movie, the trial is held in a fictitious Bible-belt town. (The real Scopes trial was in Dayton, Tennessee.) In an important subplot, the fundamentalist town preacher, whose daughter Rachael is in love with Cates, is leading a crusade against Cates. Rachael is forced (by Bradey, whom she had confided in) to reveal a conversation she had had with Cates in which he questioned God. Durham, on the other hand, is thwarted in calling the expert witnesses on evolution he has invited to the trial. At one point he is held in contempt of court. So in a final attempt, he calls on Bradey himself to be an expert witness on the *Bible*. In his cross-examination, Druham is able to show the absurdity of holding a literal interpretation of the *Bible*. In the end, Cates is found guilty but is given a fine of only $100. Bradey, who feels he has lost face because of his convoluted testimony, wants to vindicate himself and makes a speech. He dies making a speech no one is listening to after the court has been dismissed.

General Commentary

This is an excellent movie for anyone teaching about the evolution–creation debate, political and religious influences on public education, the science–religion debate, and fundamentalism. Although released in 1960, its issues are very contemporary.

Suggested Usage

Previewing Activities

- Students can research and report on the theories of creationism and evolution from different sources (such as the *Bible* and *Origin of Species*).
- Students can research and report on the real Scopes trial.
- ESL students might research and report on different types of Christianity, including fundamentalism.

Viewing Activities

GOOD PLACES TO STOP AND TALK

- Three scenes are critical for ESL students to understand. ESL teachers should stop for comprehension checks following these scenes:

    the scene in which Cates has been arrested

    the scene in which Bradey comes to town for the first time and gives a speech

    the scene in which Darrow comes to town and goes to the hotel

    Following each of these scenes students can be asked to identify who the people are and either what happened to them (Cates) or why they (Bradey and Durham) came to Hillsbore.

PATTERNS/STRUCTURES TO LOOK FOR

- ESL teachers might want to preteach some of the special courtroom language used in the film. ESL students can also be given a number of focused assignments on listening to questions, since much of the courtroom dialogue consists of questions (yes/no, "wh", and hypothetical) and answers.

Follow-up Activities

- Students can compare the facts of the movie with the facts from the real trial.
- Teachers might have students hold a debate on the theories of evolution and creationism. Students should argue the side they personally do not agree with, which will allow them to become acquainted with another perspective.
- Students can research and report on related issues. (For example: What ideas, book, or activities are not allowed in your school district?)
- Students can write about their own opinions on evolution and creationism.
- Students can find and bring in photocopies of newspaper and magazine articles printed during the real Scopes trial.
- Students can be asked to summarize Durham's arguments in writing.
- Students can research and report on the lives of William Jennings Bryan and Clarence Darrow.
- Students can research and report on what was going on domestically in the United States in 1925.
- Students can research and report on what happened to Scopes after the trial.
- Students can investigate and write their opinion of a contemporary issue involving a religious group or lobby attempting to influence a public school.

Other Considerations

None.

Ancillary Material

Lawrence, Jerome and Robert E. Lee. *Inherit the Wind.* New York: Dramatists Play Service, 1963.

Darwin, Charles. *The Origin of Species by Means of Natural Selection.* New York: F. Ungar Publishing Company, 1956.

De Camp, L. Sprague. *The Great Monkey Trial.* Garden City, N.Y.: Doubleday, 1968.

Scopes, John Thomas. *The World's Most Famous Trial.* Cincinnati: National Book Co., 1925.

Jeremiah Johnson

Subjects: 1, 16, 21, 29, 31
Playing Time: 108 minutes
Rating: PG

Director: Sydney Pollack
Producer: Joe Wizan
Date: 1972
Actor: Robert Redford

Plot Summary

Jeremiah Johnson goes into the Rockies to live as a mountain man in the last century. He meets a variety of white people (other mountain men, settlers, trappers, missionaries, and soldiers), and encounters Flathead, Blackfeet, and Crow Native Americans. He marries a Flathead woman and is raising the son of a white settler woman who went crazy. He seems content with his life. One day he is asked to escort some soldiers and a missionary into a mountain pass to rescue some settlers trapped by snow. He is pressured to go through a sacred Crow burial ground. As a result, his family is killed and he is hunted by small bands of Crow, surviving each attack to become a legend in the Rockies.

General Commentary

This interesting film fits in well with the current revisionist trend in the history of the American West. Most of the whites in this film appear to be as primitive as Native Americans are often portrayed. They are definitely not portrayed as they are traditionally— as a people who possess a more sophisticated and refined culture than Native Americans. This film would be useful for ESL, secondary, and college students studying American history, the West, Native Americans, or myths and legends.

Suggested Usage

Previewing Activities:

- Students can research the Crow and Flathead Indians and locate on a map what parts of Colorado they inhabited and where in Montana they live now.

- The teacher can promote discussion on, or ask that research be done on, what kinds of people moved West and what motivated them.

Viewing Activities

GOOD PLACES TO STOP TO TALK

- After Jeremiah Johnson marries the Indian chief's daughter is a good place to stop and talk. Teachers might ask students what they have learned about the tribe and its customs.

- Another good place to stop is after Jeremiah takes the crazy white woman's boy. Teachers may want students to speculate about why the woman wanted Jeremiah to take the boy.

- In many ways this movie is about what Jeremiah Johnson learns. Teachers can have students keep a list of the practical and cultural knowledge that Johnson learns.

- Students can also keep a list of the cultural misunderstandings they witness in the movie.

- This movie's soundtrack contains a folk song based on the legend of Jeremiah Johnson. The telling of a story in a song is a popular pattern in American English folk songs and country-western music. An ESL teacher might take the opportunity to introduce a country-western or folk song to students as an example of this.

Follow-up Activities

- A teacher can ask for written or oral commentaries on any of the following: cultural misunderstandings between the white and Native-American cultures, motivations for white people to go west, and the lives of white people on the western frontier.

- Students can write about or discuss how this movie portrays whites and Native Americans differently than they are portrayed in most westerns.

Activities for Low-Level ESL Students

The following activities are suggested for use with low-level ESL students. A teacher can:

- have students do a narration of the events up until Jeremiah Johnson meets Bear Claw.

- have students do a mute viewing of Johnson's encounter with the Indian tribe (from the time he meets them and they think he has scalped three Crows, to the time he leaves the tribe married to the chief's daughter). Teachers may ask students to write down cultural information they see about the tribe and then listen for additional cultural information.

- have students view and do a narration of the wolf attack scene.

- have students do a focused listening of the scene in which the white soldier and the preacher come to request Jeremiah's help. Teachers might have students focus their listening on how the two men request help and then convince Jeremiah to help them. What arguments do they use?

- have students do a prediction exercise at the intermission. The scene before intermission is Jeremiah looking fearful as he is returning through the Crow burial ground. Students can speculate on what Jeremiah might be afraid of.

- ask students to do a narration of the scene in which Jeremiah takes revenge on the Crow who killed his family, and then to speculate why the sole surviving Indian begins singing at him.

Other Considerations

None.

Ancillary Material

Alter, Cecil J. *Jim Bridger*. Norman: University of Oklahoma Press, 1962.

McAleur, J.F. *The Fabulous Flathead*. Polson, Mont.: Treasure State Publishing Company, 1962.

Riebeth, Carolyn Reynold. *J.H. Sharp Among the Crow Indians*. El Segundo: Upton, 1985.

JFK

Subjects: 3, 7, 15, 17, 22
Playing Time: 189 minutes
Rating: R

Director: Oliver Stone
Producers: A. Kitman Ho and Oliver Stone
Date: 1991
Actors: Kevin Costner, Sissy Spacek, Joe Pesci, Tommy Lee Jones

Plot Summary

This film is based on two books: *On the Trail of the Assassins* by Jim Garrison and *Crossfire: The Plot That Killed Kennedy* by Jim Marrs. Garrison is a district attorney from New Orleans who is convinced that the Warren Commission's Report is flawed and that Lee Harvey Oswald did not act alone. His investigation of the facts is the backbone for the movie. Characters are introduced who have connections with organized crime, the CIA, the government, and Cuba. In addition, Garrison names Lyndon Johnson and J. Edgar Hoover as unindicted co-conspirators in the death of Kennedy. The Zapruder film is used and reused to show that one gunman could not have committed the "crime of the century." Garrison's life and family are disrupted during the investigation and he almost loses everything.

General Commentary

This film will make anyone think twice about the assassination of President Kennedy. Although the film is called *JFK*, the story is about Jim Garrison and his quest for the truth. The film would be a good resource for teaching American history, American presidents, individuals who stand up against the establishment, and any of the many novels written on the assassination and its aftermath.

Suggested Usage

Previewing Activities

- Teachers may want students to research the findings of the Warren Commission.

- Teachers may have students review newspaper articles from November 1963 on the assassination and its aftermath.

- Students might review articles about the assassination and the conflicting reports given at the time.

- Teachers may have students read *On the Trail of the Assassins* by Jim Garrison.

- Teachers may also want the students to read *Crossfire: The Plot That Killed Kennedy* by Jim Marrs.

- Teachers might have students research the Bay of Pigs fiasco, knowledge of which is critical to understanding the story.

Viewing Activities

- Of the many possible scenes, the scene in which Garrison is examining the one-bullet theory might be a good place to stop and have a discussion about the same thing.

Patterns/Structures to Look For

- The courtroom scenes toward the end of the movie have excellent monologues by Garrison that are useful for focused listening with ESL students.
- The students might try to comprehend and distinguish how the southern drawls differ from other American accents.

Follow-up Activities

- Students may read a host of other books on the subject of the assassination.
- Students might research the findings of the autopsy on Governor Connally's hand, where the single bullet is supposed to be lodged.
- Students can have a formal debate on the lone-gunman theory.
- PBS did an excellent reenactment of what the trial of Lee Harvey Oswald might have been like had he lived to have one. Students can watch this as a follow-up.
- Students can research and report on what happened to Jim Garrison in his later life.

Other Considerations

The length of the movie should be considered. Occasional offensive language may disturb some students.

Ancillary Material

Garrison, Jim. *On the Trail of the Assassins*. New York: Sheridan Square Press, 1988.

Julia

Subjects:	1, 7, 14, 15, 17	**Director:**	Fred Zinnemann
Playing Time:	118 minutes	**Producer:**	Richard Roth
Rating:	PG	**Date:**	1977
		Actors:	Jane Fonda, Vanessa Redgrave, Jason Robards, Meryl Streep, Maxmillan Schell

Plot Summary

Based on a chapter in Lillian Hellman's autobiography *Pentimento, Julia* details the lifelong friendship of Lillian and her friend, Julia. Told from Lillian's point of view in a series of flashbacks, the story covers their childhood together and their school years, but concentrates on the events of an incident in 1937 when Lillian, a Jew, carried $50,000 in cash into Nazi Germany for Julia to use in her work with the anti-Nazi underground. The story ends with Lillian's quest to learn the details of Julia's death at the hands of the Nazis, and her subsequent fruitless search to find Julia's baby daughter.

General Commentary

This movie is excellent for use in a variety of classrooms and for a variety of purposes. An interesting, unfolding plot has many sub-themes that can be exploited—the life of Lillian Hellman, the American literary milieu of the 1930s, Europe before World War II, the issue of lifelong friendship, the anti-Nazi resistance, and the most disturbing question of what happened to Julia. Because the story is presented in flashbacks, the movie requires careful viewer attention. Teachers would be well advised to check for comprehension of the sequence of events presented in the movie.

Suggested Usage

Previewing Activities

- The students can read the chapter "Julia" from the book *Pentimento*.

- The students can read and report on the German resistance to Hitler, a subject that is often treated as a mere footnote in histories of the period. Specifically, students may find reading about the White Rose Society and the lives of Hans and Sophie Scholl interesting.

- The students can do encyclopedia research on the lives of Lillian Hellman and Dashiell Hammett (her lifelong lover and a prominent character in the movie). Students can use different encyclopedias and orally synthesize what they have learned.

Viewing Activities

GOOD PLACES TO STOP AND TALK

- After the scene in which young Lillian and Julia arrive at Julia's estate with Julia's grandparents is a good place for students to predict what kind of people Lillian and Julia will be when they grow up.

- After the scene in which Lillian is asked to carry the money into Germany is a good place to ask students what they would do in a similar situation.

- During the scene of the train ride into Germany is a good place for students to discuss the question: What is really happening here?

- After each flashback, students can develop an oral summary of what they have learned of Julia and Lillian. As the flashbacks progress, students should have a much clearer picture of the personalities of the two women.

PATTERNS/STRUCTURES TO LOOK FOR

- Students can watch for the many good comparisons between Lillian and Julia's relationship as children and their relationship as adults. There are also excellent comparisons between the personalities and lifestyles of the two women as adults.

- As they watch, students should develop a list of the many unanswered questions in this movie—What happened to Julia? What happened to her baby? Who was the father of her baby? Why were Julia's grandparents so insensitive?—to discuss with others at the conclusion.

Follow-up Activities

- Students can discuss the many unanswered questions in the movie and develop a list of possible answers. ESL teachers might emphasize the use of hypothetical / tentative language, such as modals and perfect modals, in discussing answers to these questions.

- Students can compare, orally or in writing, the book and the movie.

- The teacher can have students research what happened to Lillian Hellman and Dashiell Hammett and present the information to the class. An interesting discussion can be focused on the question: What information about Lillian's life that is mentioned in the movie might account for the troubles she experienced in the 1950s (when she was blacklisted by the McCarthy inquisition)?

- The teacher may have students research other mysterious stories about people who fought Nazi tyranny, including the life of Raoul Wallenberg.

- Teachers of ESL students may wish to have the students practice narration and sequencing by retelling the story (which is presented in disjointed flashbacks) of the relationship in chronological order.

- As a creative writing assignment, students can tell the rest of the story of Julia and her baby.

Other Considerations

There are no major drawbacks to using this movie, but teachers should keep in mind that because the story is told in flashback, it is important to preteach students to help them understand the sequence of the events.

Ancillary Material

Hellman, Lillian. *Pentimento*. Boston: Little Brown, 1973.

Dumbach, Annette E. *Shattering the German Night: The Story of the White Rose*. Boston: Little Brown, 1986.

Hauser, Richard. *A Noble Treason: The Revolt of the Munich Students Against Hitler*. New York: G.P. Putman, 1979.

Jens, Inge, ed. *At the Heart of the White Rose: Letters and Diaries of Hans and Sophie Scholl*. Translated by J. Maxwell Brownjohn. New York: Harper & Row, 1987.

Jurassic Park

Subjects: 1, 12, 17, 26
Playing Time: 126 minutes
Rating: PG-13

Director: Steven Spielberg
Producers: Kathleen Kennedy and Gerald R. Molen
Date: 1993
Actors: Laura Dern, Sam Neil, Richard Attenborough, Jeff Goldblum

Plot Summary

Based on Michael Crichton's novel, this blockbuster movie tells the story of a modern-day theme park that fails to open because some of the rides fail to operate correctly. The theme park, located on an island off the coast of Costa Rica, is a walk-in-the-wild-type zoo. The only problem is that the animals are dinosaurs that have been cloned from blood samples preserved in the bellies of insects preserved in amber. The movie details the visit of some investors, dinosaur experts, and children (the grandchildren of the eccentric American who developed the park) shortly before the park's opening. In a brief, 24-hour nightmare, everything goes wrong, and the movie details the not always successful efforts of the humans to keep from becoming dinosaur dinner.

General Commentary

This blockbuster movie is perhaps most famous for its incredible special effects. The dinosaurs are so lifelike that they lend an aura of authenticity to the movie. The movie shortchanges the moral issues of DNA technology and genetic engineering raised in the book, so it's best to plan on using the book with the movie. On the other hand, the movie presents what the book can only suggest, so it's a case of not one without the other.

Suggested Usage

Previewing Activities

- Students can read the book by Michael Crichton. ESL students can be directed to read the write-down of the same name, which is marketed in the juvenile literature category.

- The students can research the discovery of DNA and the development of the Human Genome Project. Students can do reports on different ways in which humans have been helped by the discoveries brought about by genetic technology. This should balance the one-sided, negative view of the subject presented in the movie and the book.

- The teacher can use the movie to teach paleontology. Students watching the movie should at least learn that there were different periods—the Jurassic was only one—and different dinosaurs. This can be assisted with resources such as the April 26th edition of *Time* Magazine and visits to local dinosaur museums and sites to find out about the dinosaurs that inhabited a particular area.

Viewing Activities

GOOD PLACES TO STOP AND TALK

- Any of the following places would be good for ESL teachers to use mute / paired / reported viewing:

    the scene in which Grant sees his first dinosaur

    the scene in which the *T. rex* attacks the car

    the scene in which the velociraptors hunt the children in the kitchen

PATTERNS/STRUCTURES TO LOOK FOR

- Much of the morality of the book is missing. Students can be directed to look for those scenes in which Malcolm (a philosopher / mathematician) and Ellie raise moral questions. This information can be used later in *Follow-up Activities*.

Follow-up Activities

- Students can compare the book and the movie.

- Students can be asked to comment, either orally or in writing, on the morality of this kind of genetic engineering. ESL students in particular can benefit from hypothetical assignments in which they answer questions (such as: What would you have done if you had been Grant in X situation?).

- Students can be asked to respond hypothetically to other genetic engineering situations. For example, what would they do if they worked for a company that wanted to make fish that were easier for fishermen to see? If they worked for a company that wanted to make square tomatoes for better packaging?

- Students can be asked to read any of the numerous articles in popular magazines from the Spring and Summer of 1993 that speculate on whether this could ever happen. They could then do oral reports on this for the class.

Other Considerations

Apart from some graphic blood-and-gore scenes, there are no special considerations to take into account when showing this movie.

Ancillary Material

Crichton, Michael. *Jurassic Park*. New York: Ballantine Books, 1991.

Crichton, Michael. *Jurassic Park: The Novelization*. New York: Putnam, 1993.

Lemonick, M.D. "Rewriting the Book on Dinosaurs." *Time*. April 26, 1993: 42–49.

The Killing Fields

Subjects:	6, 7, 15, 22, 28	**Director:**	Roland Joffee
Playing Time:	141 minutes	**Producer:**	David Puttman
Rating:	R	**Date:**	1984
		Actors:	Sam Waterson, Haing S. Ngor, John Malkovitch, Athol Fugard

Plot Summary

This is the true story of the relationship between Sidney Schanberg, a *New York Times* correspondent, and Dith Pran, his Cambodian translator. The movie begins in 1973 right after the United States has bombed a city in Cambodia. During the next two years, until their separation after the fall of Phnom Penh to the Khmer Rouge, Sydney and Dith report on the war. After the fall of Phnom Penh, Sydney returns to the United States, but Dith is trapped in what has become the killing fields of Cambodia. The second part of the film examines Dith's struggle to survive and escape and Sydney's efforts to find him. The film ends in a very emotional reunion between the two men in a refugee camp in Thailand.

General Commentary

This is an excellent film for any class studying the spread, impact, and aftermath of American involvement in Southeast Asia. Students do need some historical background to understand all that happens in this film.

Suggested Usage

Previewing Activities

- A teacher might have the students research the history of American involvement in Cambodia, as well as what happened after the fall of Cambodia to the Khmer Rouge.

- Students can locate Cambodia, Vietnam, Thailand, and the city of Phnom Penh on a map.

- Teachers might want students to research American involvement in Cambodia, including the "Nixon Doctrine."

Viewing Activities

GOOD PLACES TO STOP AND TALK

- For ESL classes, any of the military or action scenes would be good places to stop to have students do paired narrations (such as when Sidney and Dith are detained by the Khmer Rouge, and when Dith escapes from the first Khmer Rouge camp).

- The scene in which Dith leaves the embassy is the end of the first part of the movie. A teacher might have students do oral or written predictions of what they think may happen or is going to happen.

Patterns/Structures to Look For

• Students can pay careful attention to the scenes where Dith and Sydney are alone and talking. They reveal how Sydney changes. For example, in the first scene in Sydney's hotel room, Sydney shows no concern for Dith when Dith expresses fear for his family. Sydney explains that his work means everything to him. Dith agrees to stay and help Sydney. This scene and others reveal the difference between the two men. Sydney will do anything to do his job, including putting his friend in danger; Dith will do anything for his friend Sydney, including putting himself in danger.

Follow-up Activities

• Teachers may have students read the biography of Dith Pran written by Sydney Schanberg entitled *The Death and Life of Dith Pran*.

• Students can research the Cambodian holocaust or issues relating to the Cambodian refugee communities in the United States. Amnesty International is one good resource for doing this.

• A teacher might want students to find out what is happening in Cambodia today.

• Teachers can have students read the autobiography of Dr. Haing S. Ngor, who played Dith in the movie, and compare Ngor's experiences with those of Dith Pran.

Other Considerations

ESL teachers should note that one of the main characters has a heavy accent. This should not be a major obstacle, however, since the film is very visual and in many sections little dialogue is spoken. Students should be prepared to see some graphic and disturbing violence and some profanity.

Ancillary Material

Hudson, Christopher. *The Killing Fields*. London and Sydney: Pan Books, 1984.

Ngor, Haing, with Roger Warner. *A Cambodian Odyssey*. New York: Macmillan, 1987.

Schanberg, Sydney. *The Death and Life of Dith Pran*. New York: Viking. 1985.

La Bamba

Subjects:	4, 7, 10, 13, 20	**Director:**	Luis Valdez
Playing Time:	108 minutes	**Producers:**	Taylor Hackford and Bill Borden
Rating:	PG-13	**Date:**	1987
		Actors:	Lou Diamond Phillips, Esai Morales, Rosana De Soto

Plot Summary

This real-life story of singer Ritchie Valens (née Valenzuela) traces the last year of his life, in which Valens went from living in a migrant farm laborer's camp with his mother and sisters to being a national rock-and-roll star. It also examines his strained relationship with his half-brother, Bob, and his relationships with his mother and his girlfriend, Donna, who was immortalized in the song "Donna." The movie also deals with Valens' fear of flying, a fear that grew out of a tragic accident (a piece of a plane that had crashed with another plane fell onto a school yard playground and killed his best friend). Last, the movie deals with Valens' death in a plane crash.

General Commentary

This film can be used in a secondary, college, or ESL class studying the history of rock-and-roll, family relationships, or the Hispanic experience in the United States.

Suggested Usage

Previewing Activities

• The teacher can have students listen to the songs of Ritchie Valens.

• Because this is a true story the teacher can have students research the life of Ritchie Valens using library resources (such as his obituary).

Viewing Activities

GOOD PLACES TO STOP AND TALK

• After the students view the scene at the migrant labor camp, teachers might stop the film to discuss migrant farmers' work and living conditions.

PATTERNS/STRUCTURES TO LOOK FOR

• Students can focus on the differences between Ritchie and Bob and the differences between each of their relationships with their mother.

Follow-up Activities

• Students can compare and contrast the two brothers.

• Students can research the lives of the other rock-and-roll stars who went down in the plane crash (Buddy Holly and the Big Bopper). Students can find original newspaper accounts of the crash in a library.

- Teachers can have students research how Ritchie Valens fits into the history of rock-and-roll. "La Bamba" was the first rock-and-roll song not sung in English. Students can find other rock-and-roll songs sung in foreign languages (for example, "Michelle" and "Ma Belle Amie").
- Students can discuss what statement the film makes about what it means to be an "American success." Ritchie and Bob have very different experiences in America. Students can be asked to speculate as to which is more typical.

Other Considerations

ESL students may have difficulty with some of the speech, which is heavily accented, and with the occasional use of Spanish words. This should not prevent general comprehension of the story. There is also a "bump-and-grind" sex scene (albeit one with clothes on).

Ancillary Material

Mendheim, Beverly. *Ritchie Valens: The First Latino Rocker*. Tempe, Ariz.: Bilingual Press, 1987.

The Last Emperor

Subjects:	6, 7, 22	**Director:**	Bernardo Bertolucci
Playing Time:	160 minutes	**Producer:**	Jeremy Thomas
Rating:	PG-13	**Date:**	1987
		Actors:	John Lone, Joan Chen, Peter O'Toole

Plot Summary

This is the real-life story of the last emperor of the Qing Dynasty, the last dynasty of imperial China. The movie begins in a Manchurian train station in 1950 where Pu Yi, the last emperor, tries to commit suicide on his way to a Communist reeducation camp. Most of what is seen from that point on are flashbacks about his life that are sparked by interrogation sessions at the reeducation camp. Pu Yi is first seen in 1908 at the age of three when he is brought to the Forbidden City to become the emperor after the death of the Empress Dowager, Cixi. By the time he is seven, he has abdicated in favor of the new Nationalist government, but he is kept in the Forbidden City as a virtual prisoner. His only contact with the outside world is his British tutor, Reginald Flemming Johnston. Pu Yi marries and also takes a wife consort (a second wife). Eventually he leaves the Forbidden City and falls in with the Japanese, who later make him a puppet ruler of the newly formed country of Manchuguo (Manchuria). Pu Yi's personal life falls apart. He is captured by the Soviets and turned over to the Communists, who put him in a reeducation camp for war criminals for ten years. He returns to Beijing, where he works as a gardener until his death in 1967.

General Commentary

This is an excellent drama to use with students studying China in the 20th century or 20th-century world history. Even though it is a story about big issues and events, it is also a very personal story about a man who was never free and who was a victim of events he had no power to control. The movie is excellent for non-native speakers because the dialogue is clear and easy to understand. All the actors speak slowly in standard English.

Suggested Usage

Previewing Activities

- Teachers might have students study the historical events referred to in this movie (basically, the history of 20th-century China) to make comprehension of the story easier. These events include the fall of the Qing Dynasty, the Republican period, the warlord period, the Japanese invasion of China, the end of World War II, the establishment of the People's Republic of China, and the Cultural Revolution.

- Teachers might have students research life in the Forbidden City (for example, the role of eunuchs, the architecture of the Forbidden City, the costumes, and the rules and regulations).

- Teachers might have students research the many minority groups in China, paying special attention to Manchurians (the Qings were Manchurians).
- Teachers might have students do a map exercise on China, emphasizing Beijing, Tianjin, and Manchuria.

Viewing Activities

GOOD PLACES TO STOP AND TALK

- No single stopping place is critical to this movie; however, teachers might consider stopping and doing a comprehension check either before or after the interrogation / prison scenes. The interrogation / prison scenes often set up what is then depicted in flashback.

PATTERNS/STRUCTURES TO LOOK FOR

- One very obvious pattern is the historical thread that runs through this film. Teachers might have students keep track of what and how historical events affected Pu Yi's life. After the film, students can make a time-line from their notes.
- Teachers might want students to look for some patterns that repeat themselves in Pu Yi's life. Pu Yi's relationship with his mother and his wife have similar elements. Pu Yi's time in the Forbidden City and his time as a puppet of the Japanese also have similar elements. The two scenes in which doors are shut before he can escape through them are hauntingly similar.

Follow-Up Activities

- Teachers might have students compare what happened to Pu Yi with what happened to other 20th-century emperors and royalty. The Chinese use of reeducation was a unique way to deal with a fallen ruler.
- Reginald Flemming Johnston's book *Twilight in the Forbidden City* can be used to explore what Pu Yi's early life was like. Several other biographies of Pu Yi could also be used.
- In the 1980s, Pu Yi's surviving family members were interviewed by the Chinese press for English publications. Teachers can have students report on what these interviews revealed.
- Students can write or discuss their opinions on different aspects of Pu Yi's life.
- Teachers might want to invite a Chinese immigrant or visitor who lived through the Cultural Revolution to give a talk on what the Cultural Revolution was like.

Other Considerations

The movie is long. A natural breaking point is approximately halfway into the movie, when Pu Yi is forced to leave the Forbidden City.

Ancillary Material

Pu Yi, Henry. *The Last Manchu; the Autobiography of Henry Pu Yi, Last Emperor of China*. Translated by Kuo Ying Paul Tsai. New York: G.P. Putman, 1967.

Johnston, Reginald F. *Twilight in the Forbidden City*. London: V. Gollancz Ltd., 1934.

Yu, Zhuoyun, compiler. *Palaces of the Forbidden City*. New York: Viking Press, 1984.

The Last of the Mohicans

Subjects:	1, 3, 17, 21	**Director:**	Michael Mann
Playing Time:	114 minutes	**Producer:**	Hunt Lowry
Rating:	R	**Date:**	1993
		Actors:	Daniel Day Lewis, Russell Means

Plot Summary

Taken from the James Fenimore Cooper novel of the same name, this story is set in colonial America at the time of the French and Indian War (1757). Hawkeye is a scout, raised by Mohican Indians. The story opens with Hawkeye and his Indian family rescuing Cora and Alice Munro, the daughters of a British officer, after an attack by Huron Indians who side with the French. Hawkeye and his family deliver the sisters safely to their father at distant, besieged Fort William Henry. While Hawkeye is at the fort he assists colonials who have been forced to leave their families to help the British, and Colonel Munro imprisons him. Nevertheless, he makes his escape during another Indian ambush after the surrender of the fort to the French. With his family and the two British girls in tow, he is on the run across the wilderness, trying to shake off the pursuing pro-French Indians who have vowed to kill the British girls. By the end of the movie, only Cora, Hawkeye, and Hawkeye's Indian father, Chingachgook, have survived, and the latter becomes the last of the Mohicans.

General Commentary

There are earlier versions, as well as animated versions of this story. This exciting, complex, action-packed movie has so much violence that in places the blood seems to squirt onto the screen. The careful viewer will pick up on the fact that Native Americans are presented as manipulated pawns in the white man's lust for the land in colonial America. Neither the British nor the French fare well in this movie, and the only truly sympathetic characters are the American colonials, who are presented as living in a sort of romantic idyll with their Indian neighbors. While having some historical accuracy in its presentation of facts, this is definitely a revisionist telling of the way things were. Care and caution should be exercised in analyzing the film. It is most appropriate for mature, advanced-level ESL students and upper-level high school and college students.

Suggested Usage

Previewing Activities

- The students could read the novel *The Last of the Mohicans* by James Fenimore Cooper. The syntax and vocabulary are appropriate only for late high school and college levels, so a teacher may find it better to use a retelling of the original story, such as the retelling in the Globe Pacemaker Classics series.

- A class history unit on the politics of the French and Indian War would also be an excellent way to prepare to watch this film.

Viewing Activities

GOOD PLACES TO STOP AND TALK

- Due to the complex plot and dialogue, there are many places where the teacher should stop the film to check for comprehension. These include the following:

    after the point at which the colonials sign up with the British

    immediately after the first attack on Cora and Alice

    immediately after Hawkeye is jailed

    immediately after the second attack

PATTERNS/STRUCTURES TO LOOK FOR

- To keep the action in the story straight, have the students plot and chart the relationships between the following characters: Hawkeye, Hawkeye's father, Hawkeye's brother, Alice, Cora, Duncan, the British, the French, the Mohicans, the Hurons, and the colonial settlers.

Follow-up Activities

- Students can compare the story and the novel, either orally or in writing.

- The teacher could assign other books by Cooper, including *The Deerslayer*.

- The teacher could encourage students to analyze the relationships in the story (for example, the relationship of the colonials to the British and the relationship of the Indians to the colonials) to determine, based on their knowledge of history, which relationships are romanticized in the film and which are not.

- The teacher could have students analyze the role of Native Americans in this story. As shown in the film, who are the "good" Indians? Who are the "bad" Indians? What makes them "good"? What defines them as "bad"?

- The teacher could follow up with an assignment in which students write "the rest of the story" based on their knowledge of American history. What happens to Hawkeye and Cora? What happens to Hawkeye's Indian father?

- Students could research what happened to the Mohicans and other northeastern woodland Indian tribes. This information could be presented in reports. An excellent initial resource is the first chapter of Dee Brown's *Bury My Heart at Wounded Knee*. Students might research other tribes currently facing extinction to learn about what caused them to become endangered.

Other Considerations

There are a few very violent scenes in this film. The dialogue is complex and requires stopping to check for comprehension.

Ancillary Material

Cooper, James Fenimore. *The Last of the Mohicans*. Boston: Houghton, Mifflin, 1958.

Cooper, James Fenimore. *The Last of the Mohicans*. Globe Pacemaker Classics. Columbus, OH: Globe Fearon Educational Publishers.

Brown, Dee. *Bury My Heart at Wounded Knee: An Indian History of the American West*. New York: Holt, Rinehart & Winston, 1971.

Cooper, James Fenimore. *The Deerslayer*. New York: Penguin Books, 1987.

Lean on Me

Subjects:	2, 3, 4, 7, 15, 23	**Director:**	John G. Avildsen
Playing Time:	104 minutes	**Producer:**	Norman Twain
Rating:	PG-13	**Date:**	1989
		Actors:	Morgan Freeman, Beverly Todd, Robert Guillaume, Alan North

Plot Summary

This film is based on the true story of Joe Clark, an African-American high school teacher and principal from Patterson, New Jersey, who saved a high school that had deteriorated because of lack of discipline. In the 1960s, Joe is teaching at Eastside High School in New Jersey. He is a controversial teacher. Ten years later, Joe is teaching at another school when he is asked to take the principalship at his old school, Eastside High. Eastside High has become a hellhole: there is no discipline, and most of the walls are filled with graffiti and gang writing. Joe begins to "clean the place up" by wielding a baseball bat and implementing a discipline policy that would make a Marine drill instructor shudder. The result is that Joe cleans the place up both literally and figuratively.

General Commentary

Although this movie focuses on Joe Clark, it examines some of the problems lurking in our public schools. Teachers of any of the following subjects can use this film as a resource: public education in America, social problems in America, and African-American leaders. In addition, education teachers may want to show this to their students as a "what not to do" film.

Suggested Usage

Previewing Activities

• Teachers may have students explore the issue of violence in public schools.

• Students may want to express their own experiences concerning behavior, academics, drugs, and gang activity in the schools.

• Teachers may want students to collect articles about problems in schools around the country and the world.

Viewing Activities

GOOD PLACES TO STOP AND TALK

• Teachers might stop the film at any scene in which Joe confronts the problems in the school to ask any of the following questions:

  How does Joe handle the problem?

  Would you handle it that way?

  Is this guy the "Dirty Harry" of the school yard?

  What kind of person is he?

- Teachers may have the students record the ways in which Joe resolves conflicts. Students can be asked whether they like or dislike his methods and why.

Follow-up Activities

- Secondary students might videotape the goings-on in the hallways of their school and discuss what is similar and what is different from the movie.

- Secondary students might establish sister-school relationships with other schools and compare the good and bad things that happen in each system.

- Secondary teachers may want students to interview the principal of the school to see how he/she feels about the way Joe responded to problems.

- ESL teachers might want their students to compare and contrast the problems described in the movie with problems in schools in their countries.

- Teachers of future educators might want their students to discuss and react to the actions and behavior of school teachers and administrators in this film.

- Students can research, report on, discuss, and debate current developments in education reform (such as year-round schools, same-sex / same-race schools, and alternative schools).

Other Considerations

The strong language may be objectionable to some students.

Ancillary Material

Clark, Joe, with Joe Picard. *Laying Down the Law: Joe Clark's Strategy for Saving Our Schools.* Washington, D.C.: Regnery Gateway, 1989.

The Legend of Sleepy Hollow

Subjects:	5, 16, 17	**Directors:**	Jack Kinney and Clyde Geronimi
Playing Time:	33 minutes	**Producer:**	Not Listed
Rating:	G	**Date:**	year not listed
		Voice of:	Bing Crosby

Plot Summary

This short animation sticks fairly close to the short story by Washington Irving. Ichabod Crane, a schoolmaster in Sleepy Hollow, New York, is in love with Katrina van Tassel, but Katrina has a suitor—Brom Bones. One Halloween, Brom Bones decides to scare his competition out of Sleepy Hollow. At a party, he tells Ichabod the story of the mysterious Headless Horseman, who rides in the night through Sleepy Hollow. Later that night, when timorous Ichabod leaves the party, he is chased by Brom Bones disguised as the Headless Horseman. Ichabod disappears from Sleepy Hollow, and Katrina marries Brom Bones.

General Commentary

This short film is an excellent way to introduce students to the narrative and characters of one of the best-loved short stories of all time. It can be used with students of all ages and is neither childish nor offensive.

Suggested Usage

Previewing Activities

- Depending on the level of the students, the teacher can have them read the story before watching the movie or have them watch the movie before reading the story. For lower level students and ESL students, teachers would be well advised to have students read a write-down of the original story.

- Washington Irving's stories are a wonderful way to introduce students to the history of New York during the colonial period. A map exercise to acquaint students with the locale is another possibility.

- Some students may enjoy drawing the characters as they are described in the story. Pictures can later be compared to the drawings in the short film.

Viewing Activities

Good Places to Stop and Talk

- An ESL teacher can use almost any sequence to do mute / paired / reported narrations. Teachers of English-speaking students will want to show the entire film straight through.

Patterns/Structures to Look For

- If students have read the story before watching, they can look for similarities and differences between the story and the movie.

Follow-up Activities

- Students can read the short story.
- Students can compare the short story and the movie, either orally or in writing. If students drew pictures of the characters before, they can compare those to the drawings in the movie.
- Students can read other stories by Washington Irving. His writing is quite descriptive, and students often find it fun to illustrate his stories with drawings of their own.

Other Considerations

None.

Ancillary Material

Irving, Washington. *The Legend of Sleepy Hollow*, adapted by Freya Littledale. New York: Scholastic, 1992.

Irving, Washington. *Two Tales: Rip Van Winkle and the Legend of Sleepy Hollow*. San Diego: Harcourt Brace & Javonovich, 1986.

Irving, Washington. *Rip Van Winkle and Other Stories*. Longman Classics. Simplified by D.K. Swan and Michael West. White Plains, N.Y.: Longman.

The Little Mermaid

Subjects:	5, 10, 13, 17, 20, 25	**Directors:**	John Musker and Ron Clemente
Playing Time:	82 minutes	**Producers:**	Howard and John Musker
Rating:	G	**Date:**	1989
		Voices of:	Jodi Benson, Pat Carroll, Samuel E. Wright

Plot Summary

This animated story, based on the Hans Christian Andersen fairy tale, tells of Ariel, a little mermaid who wants to be human so she can marry a human prince she saved from drowning. Only two merpeople can give her the legs she wants: her father, Triton, the sea king and Ursula, the sea witch. So Ariel makes a deal with the sea witch to trade her voice for three days on land with legs. There she tries to win the prince's heart, but the sea witch bewitches him. It's a race to the finish as Ariel and her pals Sebastian, the crab and Flounder, the fish try to outdo the evil sea witch. There is a battle at the end, and unlike the fairy tale, Ariel does get her man, and they live happily every after.

General Commentary

Yes, even adults will love this fairy tale, which is anything but childish. The music is Academy-Award winning, the dialogue is snappy (particularly the running asides by Sebastian, the crab), and the story is basically that of a rebellious teenager who wants what she wants and manages to get it. The soundtrack is crystal clear and the movie lends itself particularly well to use with ESL students, many of whom come from cultures where animation is far more of an adult art form than it is here.

Suggested Usage

Previewing Activities

- Little needs to be done to preteach this film, although a teacher may want to first discuss the classical parts of any fairy tale and have students look for those parts in the story.

- The teacher may have the students read one or two different versions of the fairy tale. There are many different versions, each with a slightly different ending. In some translations, the little mermaid is portrayed as very selfless. There is a strong moral of a Christian desire for a soul, which she wants but can have only if she is loved by a human. In other versions, she is portrayed as a selfish girl, with no Christian desires, who gets what she deserves for disobeying her father. The *Follow-up Activities* will depend on the version chosen.

- An ESL teacher may do some cloze passages with the songs to prepare students to listen for them. As in all musicals, the songs contain important content. These songs in particular contain many features of natural speech, including elision and reductions.

Viewing Activities

GOOD PLACES TO STOP AND TALK

- The shipwreck scene and the scene in which Ariel sells her voice to the sea witch are excellent scenes for paired narrations.

- As a prediction exercise, teachers may stop the film just as Ariel is getting ready to swim out to the boat on which the prince is going to marry the sea witch. Students can use the future tense to predict what will happen.

PATTERNS/STRUCTURES TO LOOK FOR

- This is a movie about creatures who get others to do what they want them to do. To analyze this feature of the movie, students can be pointed toward scenes in which requests are being made. Students can be assigned by character. Some students can track Ariel; others Triton, the sea king; others Sebastian, the crab. With each, they can listen for the words and structures the character uses to make requests of others.

Follow-up Activities

- Students can compare the short stories and the movie and discuss the reasons for the differences in the versions.

- ESL students can select scenes in which requests were made and role play those scenes for additional practice with the language.

- Teachers can ask ESL students to explain how this movie would be different if it were made in their country.

Other Considerations

None. Teachers who are wary of using animated films with mature students are advised to give this a try.

Ancillary Material

Andersen, Hans Christian. *The Complete Fairy Tales and Stories*. Trans. Erik Christian Hauguard. Garden City, N.Y.: Doubleday, 1974.

Walt Disney Staff. *Little Mermaid*. New York: Viking, 1989.

The Long Walk Home

Subjects: 2, 3, 4, 23
Playing Time: 97 minutes
Rating: PG

Director: Richard Pearce
Producers: Howard W. Koch, Jr. and Dave Bell
Date: 1991
Actors: Whoopi Goldberg, Sissy Spacek

Plot Summary

The setting is Montgomery, Alabama, in 1955–1956. The bus boycott is in full swing. Rosa Parks refused to give up her seat on the bus, and Odessa Cotter has a long walk home every night. The story depicts the lives of two families. The Thompsons, a well-to-do white family, employ an African-American maid, Odessa Cotter. Odessa's family lives on the other side of town, miles away. Odessa walks to work almost every day except when Mrs. Thompson can pick her up. The story focuses on Odessa's strength to adhere to the boycott, while at the same time addressing Mrs. Thompson's political awakening to the realities of segregation.

General Commentary

This film captures a time in U.S. history that most students are aware of. But it does two things that other films have not done: it personalizes the hardship that Odessa felt, and it juxtaposes the realities that were and still are segregation. Some will criticize the film because it is told from a white person's point of view. On the other hand, it does speak to the injustices of the times and would be useful for classes studying American history and culture, as well as racism.

Suggested Usage

Previewing Activities

- Teachers may want students to research the Montgomery bus boycott.

- Teachers may assign students to research Rosa Parks and what she meant to the movement.

- The students might read a biography of Martin Luther King, Jr.

Viewing Activities

GOOD PLACES TO STOP AND TALK

- Teachers can stop the film at any of the church scenes where Odessa's family is together. Teachers may have students discuss the importance of the church to the people and the boycott.

- Teachers may want to stop the film where Odessa's older son is being beaten by three white boys and have students speculate why he does not fight back.

- Teachers might stop the film at the scene in which Mr. Thompson is attending the Citizen's Council. Students can be asked to discuss the purpose for the council and the Klanish atmosphere that exists at the meeting.

PATTERNS/STRUCTURES TO LOOK FOR

- Teachers can have students keep track of the racist remarks and note their use by certain people and their "reason" for using them.

Follow-up Activities

- Teachers can show students *Eyes on the Prize #1: Awakening (1954–1956)*, a documentary on Dr. Martin Luther King Jr.

- Teachers may want students to review old newspapers to learn how the bus boycott was covered by the press.

- Teachers may have students listen to and view the music video "Rosa Parks" by the Neville Brothers. Secondary teachers may want students to create their own video depicting that time.

- If possible, teachers may invite an eyewitness to or a participant in the events to come and speak to the class.

Other Considerations

None.

Ancillary Material

Eyes on the Prize #1: Awakening (1954–1956) (filmed documentary). Blackside, Inc. 1986.

King, Martin Luther. *Stride Toward Freedom: The Montgomery Story*. New York: Harper & Row, 1958.

Parks, Rosa, with Jin Haskins. *Rosa Parks: My Story*. New York: Dial Books, 1993.

Malcolm X

Subjects:	2, 3, 7, 15, 17, 22, 23, 24	**Director:**	Spike Lee
		Producers:	Marvin Worth and Spike Lee
Playing Time:	201 minutes	**Date:**	1993
Rating:	PG-13	**Actors:**	Denzel Washington, Angela Bassett

Plot Summary

This movie closely follows Malcolm X's life as depicted in the book *The Autobiography of Malcolm X* by Alex Haley and Malcolm X. Malcolm Little is an African-American street hustler who, after years of living a life on the fringes, is caught in a burglary and sent to jail. In jail he converts to the Nation of Islam, a black nationalist offshoot of Islam, under the direction of the Honorable Elijah Mohammed. The movie details Malcolm's rise as a leader in the religion and as an orator and leader of the black community. The story continues through his conversion to mainstream Islam and terminates with his death at the hands of gunmen from the Nation of Islam.

General Commentary

Rare is the movie that can span the entire sweep of a person's life and still be called a great movie, which this is. Historically it is accurate, following almost to the letter most of the important details mentioned in the book. From the moment the film starts, with a film clip of the Rodney King episode as an X burns into a flag and Malcolm's voice is heard, one knows that this is going to be a satisfying experience. Visually it is stunning. Denzel Washington looks and sounds so much like the real Malcolm X that in inserts of black-and-white newsreel clips, it is impossible to tell if one is watching Malcolm X or Washington playing Malcolm X. In short, the whole movie is authentic, right down to X's manner of speech, which goes from street hustler to orator. This is an appropriate movie for students in junior high, high school, and college. With extensive pre-teaching it could be used with ESL students as well.

Suggested Usage

Previewing Activities

- Students can read the book *The Autobiography of Malcolm X* by Alex Haley and Malcolm X. It is a clearly written and straightforward text; although it is long, it can be read by intermediate ESL students. At a minimum, students could read about the life of Malcolm X in an encyclopedia and then read the chapter "Mecca" from the book. This chapter tells the story of the high point of Malcolm's life.

- The movie deals with the subject of Islam, both in its mainstream form and in its heretical offshoots. Teachers can have students research the Nation of Islam and Islam to compare and contrast them. At a minimum, students could learn about the importance of the hajj (the pilgrimage to Mecca) in the life of Muslims. There is extensive coverage of Mecca in the film.

- In some public libraries, it is possible to find recordings of some of Malcolm X's speeches. Students can listen to one of these speeches and discuss it.
- One of Malcolm X's oft-quoted statements was "The white man is the devil." A teacher could lead a discussion in which students analyze what Malcolm might have meant by this sentence.

Viewing Activities

GOOD PLACES TO STOP AND TALK

- Several scenes are critical to comprehension of the action. Since many of these scenes involve actors speaking in street talk, they pose an especially difficult challenge to ESL students or any student who is not prepared to watch the movie. At a minimum, a teacher should check for comprehension during the following scenes:

    the scene in which Malcolm and his friend and his white girlfriend are brought up in front of the judge

    the scenes of Malcolm's conversion in prison, including his visitation from Elijah Mohammed

    the scene in which Malcolm learns about Elijah Mohammed's "other activities" and becomes disillusioned

    the scenes at Mecca

    Without comprehension of these scenes one cannot really understand the complete picture of who Malcolm X was.

- An ESL teacher might use any of the following scenes for mute / reported / paired narrations:

    the scene in which Malcolm gets his hair "conked"

    the scene in which Malcolm meets his white girlfriend

    the scene in which Malcolm and his friends burglarize a house

PATTERNS/STRUCTURES TO LOOK FOR

- For purposes of post-viewing discussion, students could look for the way in which Malcolm expresses his own identity as a black man and the way in which Malcolm perceives white people throughout the film.

Follow-up Activities

- Students can compare the book and the film.
- Students can do library research to find out what has happened to the Nation of Islam since Malcolm's time.
- Students can research the life and beliefs of Dr. Martin Luther King, Jr., and compare the life and beliefs of Malcolm X with those of King.

Other Considerations

The actors use authentic speech patterns, which may be difficult for ESL students to comprehend. There are some sex scenes, although the actors remain partially clothed. There is also some violence and a scene in which drugs are taken.

Ancillary Material

X, Malcolm, with assistance of Alex Haley. *The Autobiography of Malcolm X*. New York: Ballantine Books, 1993.

X, Malcolm. February 1965: *The Final Speeches*. Ed. Steve Clark. New York: Pathfinder, 1992.

The Manchurian Candidate

Subjects:	8, 17	**Director:**	John Frankenheimer
Playing Time:	126 minutes (black & white)	**Producers:**	George Axelrod and John Frankenheimer
Rating:	PG-13	**Date:**	1962
		Actors:	Laurence Harvey, Frank Sinatra, Angela Lansbury

Plot Summary

This is a Cold War tale about a young man who returns from the Korean War a hero for supposedly saving his squad members' lives. Raymond Shaw is unaware that during his captivity at the hands of Chinese and Soviet-backed North Koreans, he was brainwashed by his captors. His captors have also devised a method to control his mind once he is stateside. Shaw has been programmed to react whenever he sees a red queen in a deck of cards. Unbeknownst to Shaw, his own mother (outwardly Communist-hating but inwardly Soviet-controlled) is his "control." She instructs Shaw to assassinate the presidential nominee at the Republican national convention so his stepfather (who is also controlled by his mother) will become the presidential nominee. Shaw's former squad leader, Major Marco, realizes what is happening and is able to deprogram Shaw before the assassination. Upon realizing how he has been manipulated, Shaw kills his mother and stepfather as they sit on the nomination platform and then turns the gun on himself.

General Summary

This movie is an excellent resource for teaching about McCarthyism, the Cold War, or images of Soviet and Chinese Communism. Preteaching is absolutely necessary because many students might not understand that at one time in America, a number of people did think it was possible for a person to be brainwashed into being a communist assassin. Also the image of communists being an ever-present threat to America, an image this film is based on, was very real in many Americans' minds during the Cold War.

Suggested Usage

Previewing Activities

- Teachers might have students research and report on the Korean War, the Cold War, and McCarthyism.

- Teachers can have students read the Richard Condon novel on which this film was based.

- Students can research and report on conditioning and brainwashing theories.

Viewing Activities

- ESL teachers might want to stop and do a comprehension check after the scene in the airport which introduces Raymond, his mother, and his stepfather and presents their characters and the relationship they have with each other.

- Teachers might stop after the first dream sequence, which is a flashback to the brainwashing session, for a comprehension check. It is a strange scene and could cause some confusion if students do not understand that it was much more than a dream.

PATTERNS/STRUCTURES TO LOOK FOR

- Students can look for and describe images of Chinese, Soviets, and Communism. The film is full of images of Chinese and Soviets being godless, uncaring, evil, and willing to do anything to advance the cause of Communism.

Follow-up Activities

- There are two ways to look at this film. One is to see it as the ultimate Cold War film, and the other is to see it as a satire of the Cold War. Students can be asked to discuss and write about what they think the film was trying to say.

- Students can research further on the images Americans have had of Asians (such as the "red threat."). The documentary *Misunderstanding China* is an excellent resource for this.

- Students can compare and contrast the movie with the book.

- Teachers might have students research Cold War fears about the Communist threat by having students examine newspaper and magazine articles written during the period.

Other Considerations

None.

Ancillary Material

Condon, Richard. *The Manchurian Candidate*. New York: McGraw-Hill, 1959.

"Misunderstanding China." CBS Documentary, 1972.

M*A*S*H

Subjects:	4, 9, 19, 22	**Director:**	Robert Altman
Playing Time:	116 minutes	**Producer:**	Ingo Preminger
Rating:	R	**Date:**	1970
		Actors:	Donald Sutherland, Elliot Gould, Tom Skerritt, Sally Kellerman, Robert Duvall

Plot Summary

M*A*S*H is the story of the men and women that served in a **M**obile **A**rmy **S**urgical **H**ospital unit during the Korean War. The antiwar comedy focuses on the day-to-day lives of three doctors—Hawkeye, Trapper John, and Duke. Most of their crazy antics are directed at two other members of the unit, Maj. "Hot Lips" Hoolihan and Maj. Frank Burns. The comic relief they provide each other and the other members of the unit helps them get through the horrors they see daily. The film inspired the award-winning television series of the same name.

General Commentary

This movie does an excellent job with a difficult subject. Working at a mobile surgical hospital during a war is a bloody job, but the movie gets past the blood and into the meat of the antiwar message. Teacher dealing with the Korean War or comedy can use this film as a resource.

Suggested Usage

Previewing Activities

- Students can research the Korean War.

- Teachers might want students to create a map of Korea and Asia to use while watching the film.

- Students might ask their parents if they or anyone they knew served in the war.

- Teachers may have students research events from the recent past that deal with the MIAs from the Korean War.

Viewing Activities

GOOD PLACES TO STOP AND TALK

- Teachers may stop the film at any scene in the hospital where blood is literally covering the area. Students can be asked the following type of question: What do the doctors do to help with the horrors of the situation? Is it an escape, or is it just comedy?

- Teachers might stop the film at the scene in which the dentist is "brought back to life." Students can be asked to discuss whether this is a realistic ritual or whether the writers are poking fun at something.

- Students may be asked to note the cynicism of the three main characters. Students can discuss what type of antiwar statement their cynicism makes.

Follow-up Activities

- Teachers might invite a Korean War veteran to class to talk about the war.
- If possible, teachers might invite a current M*A*S*H* doctor to tell students what mobile hospitals are like.
- Teachers can use the scenes from the football game to have the students research racism in the military.
- Students can research and report on what kind of medical advancements came out of the M*A*S*H* units in Korea, Vietnam, and the Gulf War.

Other Considerations

The movie has some questionable language and some nudity.

Ancillary Material

Hooker, Richard. *M*A*S*H**. Mattituck, N.Y.: Amereon Ltd., 1968.

Matewan

Subjects:	3, 4, 22	**Director:**	John Sayles
Playing Time:	100 minutes	**Producers:**	Pegg Rajski and Maggie Renzi
Rating:	PG	**Date:**	1988
		Actors:	Chris Cooper, Mary McDonnell

Plot Summary

This drama is based on a real event that occurred in Matewan, West Virginia, in 1920. A labor organizer, Joe, comes to town to help coal miners who have gone out on strike. He convinces the African-American and Italian immigrants who are scab miners to join the strike. Eventually most of the miners are forced out of the homes because the coal company holds their leases. They camp together outside of town. Most of the miners want to fight back against the company, but Joe cautions them to be nonviolent. One miner tries to betray the cause and convinces a girl who likes Joe to make up a lie about him. The film ends with the bloody Matewan massacre. Joe dies trying to stop it; a woman who befriended him kills the worst of the company's hired guns; and her son, the narrator of the story, turns away from preaching the Gospel to preaching the union message.

General Commentary

This is an excellent resource for teaching about the American labor movement. Specifically this movie tells the story of the beginning of, as the narrator says, "the great Coal Field Wars" of West Virginia.

Suggested Usage

Previewing Activities

- Teachers can have students research and report on different aspects of the American labor movement (such as its origins, its setbacks, its leaders, its controversies, its history, etc.).
- Students can locate Matewan on the map of West Virginia. They will notice that it is in the southwest of the state, which is referred to on several occasions in the film.

Viewing Activities

GOOD PLACES TO STOP AND TALK

- Because the accents in this film are somewhat heavy, ESL teachers might want to stop each time a major character is introduced and speaks to make sure students know who the person is. The important characters are: Joe, the labor organizer; the woman who owns the boarding house and befriends Joe; her son; the leader of the white miners who ends up betraying the cause; the leader of the African-American miners; the leader of the Italian miners; the two company-hired guns; the sheriff; and the mayor.

- A good place for ESL teachers to stop for a comprehension check is the scene at the first union meeting, right after the leader of the African-American miners speaks and then Joe speaks about how once a man is a union member, other members must treat him equally. This scene establishes some of the basic ideas central to the film.

- A whole series of scenes related to the attempted betrayal of Joe rely on listening to whispers and understanding inferences. ESL teachers might use these scenes for either listening activities or for a comprehension check.

PATTERNS/STRUCTURES TO LOOK FOR

- Throughout the film, two opposing forces affect the coal miners and their families' lives: the company and the union. Students can list and describe ways that the company affected the lives of the people of Matewan and the ways the union, or at least the idea of the union, affected their lives.

Follow-up Activities

- Teachers might want students to research and report on what happened after the Matewan massacre.

- Teachers can have students research and report on other well-known American labor disputes.

- Teachers might want to introduce students to union songs, which are used as a form of protest. The movie begins with such a song.

- Teachers might want students to read the novel *Storming Heaven*, which is an account of another West Virginia mining war.

Other Considerations

The accents are very heavy throughout this film. ESL teachers might want to do more preteaching on the Matewan massacre to assist comprehension.

Ancillary Material

Corbin, David Allen. *Life, Work, and Rebellion in the Coal Fields: the Southern West Virginia Miners, 1800–1922.* Urbana: University of Illinois Press, 1981.

Giardina, Denise. *Storming Heaven.* New York: W.W. Norton Company, 1987.

Lee, Howard B. *Bloodletting in Appalachia; the Story of West Virginia's Four Major Mine Wars and Other Thrilling Incidents of its Coal Fields.* Morgantown: West Virginia University, 1969.

Lunt, Richard D. *Law and Order Vs. the Miners, West Virginia 1907–1933.* Hamden, Conn: Archon Books. 1979.

Seeger, Pete, and Bob Reiser. *Carry It On! The Story of America's Working People in Song and Picture.* Bethlehem, Penna: Sing Out, 1991.

Missing

Subjects:	13, 14, 22	**Director:**	Costa Gavras
Playing Time:	122 minutes	**Producers:**	Edward and Mildred Lewis
Rating:	PG	**Date:**	1982
		Actors:	Sissy Spacek, Jack Lemmon

Plot Summary

What really happened to Charlie Horman? Charlie Horman is a nice American boy living the laid-back, leftist, ex-patriot lifestyle in Santiago, Chile, with his wife, Beth, at the time of the coup against Salvadore Allende in 1973. Charlie happens to be in Vina, where the coup starts, when it starts, and he realizes who's really behind the coup: the U.S. government. Charlie goes back to Santiago, accompanied by an American officer, and promptly disappears from his home. He's never seen again. This movie tells the story of Beth's and his father's efforts to find out what happened to Charlie, and their realization that it was really U.S. operatives in Chile who kidnapped and killed him. It's also the story of his father's realization that America might be wrong and his son might have been right. At the end of the movie, Charlie's body is sent to the United States.

General Commentary

Missing has suspense, mystery, a father-son story, and a blatant condemnation of the United States and its role in Latin America. All of this is well directed by the political director Costa Gavras and more than convincingly acted by Spacek and Lemmon. The movie could be used with students from junior high through college, as well as with ESL students.

Suggested Usage

Previewing Activities

- Students who know nothing about the 1973 coup against Allende will be at a loss to understand this movie. Teachers will want to preteach the concepts of coup, Allende, and Pinochet, at least by encyclopedia research.

- Teachers may wish to use this movie as an opportunity to introduce students to the poetry of Pablo Neruda, particularly some of his protest poetry regarding the Chilean revolution.

- Local branches of Amnesty International (see the phone book) may have reports on human rights abuses in Chile at the time of the coup and in the years following the coup. Teachers may have students read and report on it.

- As a preteaching or a follow-up activity, teachers may have students read the *New York Times* reporting on the disappearance of Charlie Horman as well as the white paper that the U.S. State Department released pointing out the "errors" in the movie's reporting of the facts.

Viewing Activities

• A few scenes are critical for comprehension. These scenes include: all flashback scenes about the time in Vina and the disappearance; and the scenes in which Charlie's father and Beth talk to the man at the Ford Foundation and the military officer who has taken refuge at an embassy. Teachers may wish to do comprehension checks after these scenes.

PATTERNS/STRUCTURES TO LOOK FOR

• This is, in part, a story of a father coming to accept what his son was and to reject what his country has become. Students can be told to track Mr. Horman's attitude toward his son, his attitude toward his country, and how those attitudes change as he learns the truth.

Follow-up Activities

• The teacher might lead a discussion on the topic: Who Killed Charlie Horman? This could also be turned into a creative writing journalism assignment.

• The teacher may have students compare the facts as they are presented in the *New York Times*, in the movie, and in the white paper issued by the U.S. State Department.

Other Considerations

There are scenes depicting mass incarceration and tortured, mutilated people.

Ancillary Material

Articles reporting on Charlie Horman can be found in the following issues, pages, and columns of the *New York Times*. September 23 (1:2), 25 (46:4), 27 (4:4); October 5 (7:1), 8 (10:4), 20 (9:3), 31 (3:5); and November 19 (20:4), all 1973.

"U.S. Takes Issue with Costa-Gavras Film on Chile." *New York Times*. Feb. 10, 1982 (22:3).

Mississippi Burning

Subjects: 3, 4, 7, 22, 23
Playing Time: 125 minutes
Rating: R

Director: Alan Parker
Producer: Fredrick Zollo
Date: 1988
Actors: Gene Hackman, Willem Dafoe

Plot Summary

This movie tells the story of two FBI men who are investigating the disappearance of three civil rights workers in Jessup County, Mississippi, in 1964. Mr. Ward, the younger man, is the boss, and he's a by-the-book Northerner with a great deal of sympathy for the civil rights movement. Mr. Anderson, the older man, is the former sheriff of a small southern town, with a great deal of understanding of how the good-ole'-boy network works. Together the two set out to find out what happened to the three civil rights workers. Mr. Anderson's good-ole'-boy strategy of courting the wife of a deputy that he suspects of having been involved with the disappearance eventually provides the tip-off that the men need to find the bodies. Mr. Ward comes to realize that the by-the-book method isn't going to work to round up the guilty parties—several of whom are prominent law and civil authorities who are members of the Klan—so he agrees to the more "down home" approach that Mr. Anderson uses. They get their men.

General Commentary

Anyone who remembers the time period in which this film is set will quickly realize that this movie brings revisionism to new heights. The FBI as a pro-civil rights organization? Spending limitless amounts of time, money, and manpower to find out what happened to two Jewish college students and an African-American? Despite the fact that this movie puts a very pro-FBI twist on things, it does manage to capture the intensity of the time, and the heat (literally and figuratively) of the period. It does this by setting up clear lines: northern and southern, good and bad, white and black, F.B.I. and Klan. The lines work to tell the story, but one should never lose sight of the fact that this is a story and has been represented in the way the storytellers wish. As a focus piece for students to use to find out what really happened, it works for students in high school, college, and advanced ESL.

Suggested Usage

Previewing Activities

- Certain concepts are vital to understanding the background presented in this story. These concepts include Selma, Montgomery, Oxford, Ole' Miss, civil rights movement, voter registration, segregation, and, of course, the Ku Klux Klan. At a minimum, the teacher should have the students look these words up in an encyclopedia and present what they have learned to each other. It is particularly important to understand the connections between these words.

- Other suggested activities to teach these concepts include: library research to find authentic newspaper accounts (from both northern and southern newspapers); viewing of documentaries, including the award-winning *Eyes on the Prize*; and reading famous civil rights classics such as Martin Luther King, Jr's.' "Letter from the Birmingham Jail."

Viewing Activities

GOOD PLACES TO STOP AND TALK

- The many excellent scenes that an ESL teacher could use for a mute / reported / paired narration include the following:

    the first scene, in which people use segregated water fountains

    the scene in which the civil rights workers are followed and shot

    the many different scenes in which burnings / hangings / attempted hangings take place

- A few scenes are critical to comprehension. Teachers may wish to do comprehension checks after the following:

    the scene in which Ward and Anderson introduce themselves to each other (This scene is particularly useful for students to predict the different ways in which these two men will approach their investigation.)

    the scene in which the deputy's wife tells Anderson about the bodies

    the scene in which the mayor is threatened by the black FBI agent

PATTERN/STRUCTURES TO LOOK FOR

- A very big part of this movie is the difference in style between the two men. Half of the students can be asked to track how Ward interacts with the people of the town, and the other half can be asked to track how Anderson interacts. Students should be told to look for differences in how the two men approach people to get information and what methods they use when they are unable to get information.

Follow-up Activities

- The teacher can lead a discussion in which they ask students to explain the differences between the styles of the two men and give their opinion as to which was most effective.

- The teacher may wish to have students analyze the images of people that the movie presents. How are Northerners presented as opposed to Southerners? How is the FBI presented as opposed to the Klan?

- Students are often interested in the subject of the Klan, and they may wish to investigate this subject and report on it to the class. One good resource on the group's activities is the civil rights organization, Southern Poverty Law Center.

- Teachers can have students research the role the FBI played in the activities of the era and compare the FBI's role as it is presented in the movie with the role revealed in their research.

Other Considerations

This is a violent movie about violent times. There are some scenes of barbaric brutality, including a hanging, a castration (off camera), and a spouse beating.

Ancillary Material

Garrow, David J. *Protest at Selma: Martin Luther King and the Voting Rights Act of 1965.* New Haven, Conn: Yale University Press, 1978.

Harkey, Ira B. *The Smell of Burning Crosses; an Autobiography of a Mississippi Newspaperman.* Jacksonville, Ill: Harris-Wolfe, 1967.

King, Martin Luther. *A Testament of Hope: The Essential Writing of Martin Luther King.* Ed. James Melvin Washington. San Francisco: Harper & Row, 1986.

Williams, Juan. *Eyes on the Prize: America's Civil Rights Year 1954–1965.* New York: Viking, 1987.

Moscow on the Hudson

Subjects:	4, 9, 25	**Director:**	Paul Mazursky
Playing Time:	115 minutes	**Producer:**	Paul Mazursky
Rating:	R	**Date:**	1984
		Actors:	Robin Williams, Maria Conchita Alonso

Plot Summary

This is a comedy about a Russian saxophone player, Vladimir Ivanoff, who works for a Moscow circus. On a Soviet-sponsored tour to New York, Vladimir defects while visiting Bloomingdales department store. The film portrays his life in the Soviet Union as one of shortages and pressure from his boss, a government official. The film also explores his struggle to find work and happiness in New York City. He comes in contact with many people who have come to New York from another area of the United States or from another country—China (the reporter who covers his defection); Italy (a Bloomingdale's clerk who becomes his girlfriend); Alabama (the African-American security guard at Bloomingdales who later becomes his closest friend); Cuba (his immigration lawyer); Korea (a taxicab driver); the Caribbean (the Immigration and Naturalization officer worker who processes his case); and Texas (a customer in Vladimir's limousine).

General Commentary

This is an excellent film to show if teaching about modern immigrants to the United States and/or what it is like to be a foreigner. It also can be used to explore stereotypes of Russians. This film is recommended for secondary or ESL audiences as a tool for thought and discussion on the subjects mentioned previously in this section.

Suggested Usage

Previewing Activities

- The teacher can have students look up the words *defection* and *political asylum* and discuss their meanings. Students can also research known defections (such as Baryshnikov) and the reasons for the defections.

- The teacher can have students research the general history of immigration in the United States, with particular emphasis on immigration to New York.

Viewing Activities

GOOD PLACES TO STOP AND TALK

- The scene in which Vladimir's Russian friend Anatoly, who had planned to defect but was unable to, is looking at Vladimir and flapping his arms like a bird is a turning point in the film. Teachers can have students predict what might happen next.

- The most obvious pattern to have students look for is the types of people Vladimir meets in New York. Students can list the different people Vladimir encounters, where they came from, and why they came to New York.

Follow-up Activities

- ESL students can discuss orally or in writing what it was like when they first came to this country, what their expectations of the United States were, and whether those expectations were fulfilled.

- Freedom becomes an important idea to Vladimir during the course of the movie. Students can discuss orally or in writing what the word meant to Vladimir and his friend Anatoly and what it means to students.

- Students can interview people who are visiting, studying, or have immigrated to the United States and make reports on how they felt when they first came to the United States and how they feel now.

- Students can do follow-up research on the ethnic neighborhoods that make up New York City (such as Chinatown, Jamaica, Little Italy, etc.).

Other Considerations

ESL teachers should note that the first part of this movie is in subtitles, and that once Vladimir gets to New York almost everyone he encounters has a different accent. None of these affect the general comprehension of the story. Secondary teachers should note that there are two rather graphic sex scenes, one at the beginning and one at the end of the story.

Murder on the Orient Express

Subjects: 1, 11, 17
Playing Time: 127 minutes
Rating: PG

Director: Sidney Lumet
Producers: John Brabourne, Richard Goodwin, and Robert F. Colesberry
Date: 1974
Actors: Albert Finney, Lauren Bacall, Jaqueline Bisset, Martin Balsam, Michael York, John Gielgud, Vanessa Redgrave, Wendy Hiller, Sean Connery, Anthony Perkins, Ingrid Bergman, Richard Widmark

Plot Summary

This whodunit, based on the Agatha Christie mystery, concerns a murder on the famous Orient Express train as it sits snowbound in the mountains on its way from Istanbul to France. Any one of a dozen passengers on the train could be the murderer. Hercule Poirot, who also happens to be on the train, learns that all have connections to a famous Armstrong kidnapping case (quite similar to the Lindbergh case) and that the murdered man was the kidnapper who got away.

General Commentary

This is a lavish production, with no expense spared to get the finest actors, set, and script. Properly taught, it could be a vehicle to explore the famous Lindbergh kidnapping, the history of the train, or the story itself. It's a highly recommended movie for all audiences from high school through college, and intermediate and advanced ESL students.

Suggested Usage

Previewing Activities

- The students could read the story, but if they do, they should *not* read the ending until they've seen the movie.

- Students could research and report on the Lindbergh kidnapping via newspaper accounts from the time (1932).

- The teacher could have students research and report on the history of this famous train. A travel agent can provide information about the route, which would make an excellent map exercise. Students could investigate other authors who have written about this train, including Graham Greene.

Viewing Activities

GOOD PLACES TO STOP TO TALK

- It's an excellent idea to stop the tape after Poirot interviews each of the suspects to ask students: Do you think this person might be the murderer? Why or why not?

- As each person is being interviewed, students can consider the attitude he/she displays toward the interview.

Follow-up Activities

- Students can compare the book and the movie.

- The students can compare the story to another multiple-suspect story by Agatha Christie—*Ten Little Indians*.

- Students can research and report on what happened to Bruno Hauptmann, the convicted kidnapper in the Lindbergh case, and the controversy that surrounded and continues to surround his trial and execution. This makes a nice contrast to the justice meted out in *Murder on the Orient Express*.

- Students can research and report on what happened to the Lindbergh family, on whom the Armstrong family was modeled, and decide whether they would have been like the Armstrong family in seeking revenge.

Other Considerations

None.

Ancillary Material

Christie, Agatha. *Murder on the Orient Express*. London: Collins, 1968.

Christie, Agatha. *Ten Little Indians*. New York: Dodd Mead, 1978.

Fisher, Jim. *The Lindbergh Case*. New Brunswick: Rutgers University Press, 1987.

My Left Foot

Subjects:	7, 13, 15, 17	**Director:**	Jim Sheridan
Playing Time:	103 minutes	**Producer:**	Noel Pearson
Rating:	R	**Date:**	1989
		Actors:	Daniel Day-Lewis, Brenda Fricker, Alison Whelan

Plot Summary

This is the biography of Christy Brown. Stricken from birth by cerebral palsy, he is able to control only one part of his body—his left foot. The movie starts with Christy as a young boy in Dublin. Although poor, his family is very loving and his brothers play with him without concern for his handicap. One day Christy shows his family that he can write with his foot. From this point on he is encouraged to learn, paint, and write. As Christy gets older he begins to write poetry, novels, and he even paints. It is obvious that Christy is a genius. This, however, make Christy a very hard man to live with. He begins drinking and eventually becomes an alcoholic. His writings and paintings are what keep him going, but in real life, the alcohol eventually leads to his death.

General Commentary

This outstanding film could be used for many classes. Teachers teaching about psychology, the disabled, and individual courage can use this film as a resource.

Suggested Usage

Previewing Activities

- Students might research and report on how handicapped people have been and are treated in the United States and other countries.

- Teachers may have students view the artwork and/or read the poetry of Christy Brown.

- Students may be asked to research the Irish-British conflict, which is alluded to on several occasions in the film.

Viewing Activities

GOOD PLACES TO STOP AND TALK

- The teacher might stop the movie when Christy's father is at the bar after Christy has been born. The father toasts his son and vows that he will never live in an institution. Students can speculate on what kind of life Christy may have.

- Teachers might stop the film at the scene in which Christy picks up the chalk with his left foot. Students can try to do this themselves.

PATTERNS/STRUCTURES TO LOOK FOR

- Students might look for the pattern of self-destruction that Christy develops as he gets older.

Follow-up Activities

- Students may be asked to report on the laws that are in place to protect and assist the handicapped.
- Teachers may invite a handicapped person to class to tell of the struggle he/she has gone through.
- Secondary teachers might include children from the special needs area in the class and have volunteers assist them with lessons.
- Students can find an obituary on Christy Brown. Students can summarize information from the obituary that was not provided in the film.
- Students can research the causes and effects of cerebral palsy.

Other Considerations

There is limited use of profanity. ESL teachers may wish to note the many strong Irish accents of characters in the movie.

Ancillary Material

Brown, Christy. *Collected Poems*. London: Secker and Warburg, 1982.

Brown, Christy. *A Promising Career*. London: Secker and Warburg, 1982.

Connaughton, Shane, and Jim Sheridan. *My Left Foot*. London and Boston: Faber & Faber, 1989.

Nicholas and Alexandra

Subjects:	7, 14, 17, 22, 30	**Director:**	Franklin J. Schaffner
Playing Time:	183 minutes	**Producer:**	Sam Spiegel
Rating:	GP	**Date:**	1971
		Actors:	Michael Jayston, Lawrence Olivier, Jack Hawkins, Janet Suzman, Alexander Knox, John Wood, Tom Baker

Plot Summary

This epic story of the fall of the Russian Empire examines the life of Czar Nicholas II and his wife, Alexandra. The history of Russia from the late 1890s to the death of the Romanovs is chronicled closely. The film concentrates on the family life—the hemophiliac son, the influence of Rasputin, and other things that distract Nicholas from governing properly. The film covers events prior to World War I, events during the war, the collapse of the Czarist government, the Kerensky government, the Bolshevik Revolution, and the death of the Romanov family.

General Commentary

"Spectacular" is the word to sum up the cinematography. This film is indeed a pleasure to watch. It is also an excellent history of the time and could assist a teacher teaching about the 20th century, the establishment of the former Soviet Union, world leaders, and/or Russia. The novel by Robert K. Massie may also help students understand the movie. It is also important to note that the film has been edited by an educational resource group and is available in three 30-minute segments as well as the original three hours and three minutes.

Suggested Usage

Previewing Activities

- Teachers might have the students research the time period and create time lines of the events.
- Teachers may want to list the personalities of the time and have students write short biographies of one or all.
- Teachers might want students to research hemophilia.
- Teachers can have students study the Romanovs.

Viewing Activities

GOOD PLACES TO STOP TO TALK

- It is a good idea to stop and talk about the significance of each character as he/she is introduced.

- The relationship between Alexandra and Rasputin is interesting. Students might note the events that bring these two together and how this relationship helps in undermining the czar.

- Teachers may have the students look for characteristics of Nicholas's behavior that helped lead to the end of the Romanov Dynasty.

Follow-up Activities

- The teacher may ask students why they think all the Romanov family was shot.

- The teacher may have students pick either Nicholas or Alexandra and write an obituary for a newspaper.

- The teacher could have the students read Tolstoy's "After the Ball" and compare the brutality in it to the scenes from the movie.

- Teachers can have students research and report on theories that suggest that at least one of the Romanovs survived the assassination.

- Students can research the recent interest in the Romanovs in Russia.

- Students can read the novel and compare it to the movie.

Other Considerations

The film is long, so teachers will need to block time to show it. Also, the graphic firing squad scene at the end may disturb some students.

Ancillary Materials

Massie, Robert K. *Nicholas and Alexandra*. New York: Antheneum, 1967.

Tolstoy, Leo. "After the Ball." *Introduction to Great Books, 2nd Series*. Chicago: The Great Books Foundation, 1990.

An Officer and a Gentleman

Subjects:	19, 25	**Director:**	Taylor Hackford
Playing Time:	126 minutes	**Producer:**	Martin Efland
Rating:	R	**Date:**	1982
		Actors:	Richard Gere, Debra Winger, Louis Gossett, Jr., David Keith

Plot Summary

This love story has the unusual setting of a Naval Air Corps Officer's Candidate School. Zack Mayo and Sid Worley enter officer's school with the dream of becoming navy fliers. Zack finds that the drill instructor, Sgt. Emil Foley, is determined to make him drop out. During the months spent at the school, Zack and Sid meet two local women, Paula and Lynette. Zack and Paula become lovers, as do Sid and Lynette. Paula and Lynette begin to think that Zack and Sid are like the previous candidates at the school, whose motto was "Love them and leave them." Despite the continual harassment by Sgt. Foley and the up-and-down love affair with Paula, Zack makes it through. To show that he is a gentleman, he even comes back to carry Paula off as the movie ends. Sid, however, is duped by Lynette and tragically commits suicide.

General Commentary

This movie does a good job of portraying life in Officer's Candidate School. The role of drill instructor (played by Louis Gossett Jr.) was based on an actual drill instructor. Teachers teaching about the military can use this film as a resource.

Suggested Usage

Previewing Activities

• Teachers may have students visit an ROTC center, a base, or a recruiting office and interview military personnel on what it takes to get into OCS.

Viewing Activities

GOOD PLACES TO STOP AND TALK

• Any scene in which Foley challenges Zack is a good place to stop and discuss whether Foley is harassing Zack or whether he is trying to make him a better candidate.

PATTERNS/STRUCTURES TO LOOK FOR

• The teacher may have students look for the stereotypical behavior (such as sexist comments) of characters in the movie.

• Teachers may want students to look for specific patterns of speech used by military personnel.

Follow-up Activities

- The teacher may have the students discuss the role of the sexes in the military.
- Teachers also may have the students review the film to identify the sexist attitudes that are evident throughout the movie
- Students can explain how they think the movie created a positive image of the military.
- Secondary teachers can have students create a poster promoting OCS.
- Teachers may want to invite officers into class to discuss whether they think the movie was a realistic portrayal of OCS.
- Teachers can have students discuss, orally or in writing, how Zack changes from the beginning to the end of the film.

Other Considerations

There are scenes with nudity, and some language may be offensive. The suicide scene, although brief, may disturb the students.

Oliver!

Subjects:	17, 20	**Director:**	Carol Reed
Playing Time:	145 minutes	**Producer:**	John Woolf
Rating:	G	**Date:**	1968
		Actors:	Mark Lester, Hugh Griffith, Jack Wild, Ron Moody, Coral Browne, Oliver Reed, Shani Wallis, Ron Secombe

Plot Summary

This is the classic Dickens story of Oliver Twist, an orphan who would rather be anyplace other than the orphanage or the foster families he is placed with. He "bumbles" his way out of the orphanage and meets another street kid, the Artful Dodger. Dodger introduces him to Fagan, who runs a pickpocket ring, and before Oliver knows what has happened, he is considered "part of the family." His attempts at pickpocketing are poor, and he is caught and taken to court. Saved from prison by a wealthy gentleman, he gets a look at how the other side lives. But it is not long before his old "family" comes looking for him and takes him away. Oliver eventually returns to the wealthy old gentleman, and the law breaks up Fagan's "family of thieves."

General Commentary

This musical rendition of *Oliver Twist* tends to lighten the harshness of 19th-century England, but at the same time the tenderness helps students sympathize with the plight of the orphan. This film's depiction of a pickpocket "family" in 19th-century Britain is relevant to 20th-century American gang "families." There are many possibilities for which this film could be used, but students studying English literature and English history will find it entertaining and valuable.

Suggested Usage

Previewing Activities

- The teacher could get the lyrics to the songs in the movie so the students can examine how the lyrics tell a story. Teachers can have students predict what a particular scene will be like from listening to the lyrics of the song.

- Teachers may want to have students read *Oliver Twist* by Charles Dickens and think about why Dickens might have written the novel.

- Students can research what life in London was like during the time the story takes place.

Viewing Activities

GOOD PLACES TO STOP AND TALK

- Many scenes provide great insights into life in Britain at the time the story takes place. For example, teachers can stop the film at the scene in which Mr. Bumble is selling Oliver as if he were an animal and have students speculate on the rights of children at that time.

- One scene that may generate a good discussion on gang behavior and acceptance is the one in which Dodger and Oliver sing "Consider Yourself One of the Family." Teachers might want students to discuss how Oliver is made to feel at home in this scene.

PATTERNS/STRUCTURES TO LOOK FOR

- The film's lyrics may provide students with an opportunity to explore the relationship between lyrics and dialogue and how the two are used to complement each other throughout the film.

Follow-up Activities

- The students may research the children's rights movement to find out how society has progressed since the time *Oliver Twist* was written.

- The students may want to compare the laws regarding child labor in the United States with those of Great Britain and other countries.

- Teachers may have musically talented students write a song with lyrics that help expose a problem faced by children today (For example: "Luka" by Suzanne Vega).

- Students can research and report on how the Industrial Revolution affected the lives of people living in American and European cities.

Other Considerations

This film is rather long and at times is a bit slow. The movie could be shown in two days. The 153-minute playing time may present some problems.

Ancillary Material

Ackroyd, Peter. *Dicken's London: An Imaginative Vision*. London: Headline Book Publishing Co. 1987.

Dickens, Charles. *Oliver Twist*. Oxford: Clarendon, 1966.

Platoon

Subjects: 4, 10, 18, 19, 28
Playing Time: 120 minutes
Rating: R

Director: Oliver Stone
Producer: Arnold Kopelson
Date: 1986
Actors: Tom Berenger, Johnny Depp, Willem Dafoe, Keith David, Charlie Sheen, Kevin Dillon

Plot Summary

This is a story about a young man, Chris, who goes to Vietnam in 1967 and whose life is transformed by what he experiences. Included in these experiences are: Chris' struggle between keeping a sense of morality (following his squad leader, Elias) and abandoning all sense of what he knows is right (following his sergeant, Barnes); his involvement in what could have been another My Lai massacre; and finally his survival of a horrific battle in which almost everyone else dies. The story is told in two ways: through the central character's narration of letters he writes to his grandmother and through the portrayal of his time in Vietnam.

General Commentary

This is an excellent movie for students studying America's involvement in Vietnam and America's own internal conflict regarding Vietnam. It is also useful for examining visual and figurative metaphors. Although this movie can be used for secondary, ESL, or college students, note the points mentioned in *Other Considerations* below.

Suggested Usage

Previewing Activities

- Students can locate Vietnam and the Vietnamese / Cambodian border on a map and study the physical geography of the region. All the action in this film takes place in a terrain unfamiliar to most American students.

- Teachers can have students look up the words *platoon* and *squad* and distinguish between them.

- Students can look up newspaper accounts of the My Lai massacre. A scene in the movie relates indirectly to that event.

- Students can investigate what kinds of young men went to Vietnam. What social and economic classes were overrepresented and underrepresented?

- Teachers might introduce the idea of visual and spoken metaphor to their students.

Viewing Activities

GOOD PLACES TO STOP AND TALK

- ESL teachers might want to stop after Chris narrates his first letter and make sure students understand what has been said (For example: Who is this young man? Who is he writing to? Why did he decide to go to Vietnam?).

- Because students might want to discuss what they have seen after the very disturbing village scene, teachers can ask students to retell what happened, to explain why people did the things they did, to discuss how they (the students) feel about what they have seen, and to discuss what they (the students) might have done if they had been there.

PATTERNS/STRUCTURES TO LOOK FOR

- This film is loaded with metaphoric references. In the first scene, the plane opening up to unload the new soldiers is a visual metaphor for birth. The main character sees a snake in the jungle, a visual metaphor for the temptation he is about to undergo. Elias and Barnes become symbols of good and evil battling for Chris's soul. Barnes' death scene uses the visual metaphor of crucifixion. The battle between Barnes and Elias can also be viewed as a metaphor for the internal conflict that Americans experienced in America regarding the Vietnam War. Further, the fact that Vietnamese soldiers are rarely seen in this film, and that often the Americans appear as though they are fighting shadows and each other, are visual metaphors for an unknown enemy. Students can be asked to identify as many symbols / metaphors as they can while viewing the movie.
- Students can list and describe the different types of men Chris meets. Students can be asked to explain the the men's different motivations and their different ways of dealing with the war.

Follow-up Activities

- Students can research newspaper accounts about the Vietnam War.
- A teacher can invite a Vietnam veteran to talk to the students about his/her own experience in the war, or students can be asked to interview a Vietnam veteran about his/her own experience.
- Students can research drug abuse by American soldiers in Vietnam, and the overrepresentation of minorities in the American military during the Vietnam War.
- A teacher might follow up this movie by having students read passages from *Dear America: Letters Home from Vietnam*.
- Students can write on how Chris changes from the beginning of the movie to the end of the movie.

Other Considerations

This movie is very violent and contains some very disturbing scenes, as well as a lot of vulgarity. Secondary teachers should consider this before using the movie. ESL teachers should note that because of the vulgarity and slang, ESL students may find it difficult to understand dialogue, but not the movie in general. The screenplay is available (see Ancillary Material).

Ancillary Material

Stone, Oliver, and Richard Boyle. *Oliver Stone's "Platoon" and "Salvador."* New York: Vintage Books, 1987.

Bilton, Michael, and Kevin Sin. *Four Hours in My Lai.* New York: Vintage, 1992.

Edelman, Bernard. *Dear America: Letters Home from Vietnam.* New York: W.W. Norton, 1985.

Pow Wow Highway

Subject: 21
Playing Time: 91 minutes
Rating: R

Director: Jonathan Wacks
Producer: Jan Wieringa
Date: 1989
Actors: A Martinez, Gary Farmer

Plot Summary

This adventure road-trip movie portrays two Cheyenne Native Americans, Buddy Red Bow and Philbert Bono, on a trip from Montana to Arizona to help Buddy's sister who has been framed for possession of drugs in order to get Buddy out of town during a crucial vote on an issue he opposes on the reservation. The story, however, is really about what it means to be a Native-American man. Three are portrayed. Buddy is the still-angry American Indian Movement activist. Philbert is a dreamer and spiritual seeker looking for his future in his cultural past. The third Native-American man is an old friend of Buddy's, who was once an activist like Buddy. He has given up on the reservation (in his case, the Pine Ridge Sioux reservation) and needs to hitch a ride for himself and his wife off the reservation to Denver, where they are moving.

General Commentary

This interesting little film looks at a section of American culture that is rarely dealt with in movies. Secondary, college, and ESL students studying Native Americans can benefit from seeing the movie, which raises many interesting questions. For example: What does it mean to be a Native American today, and how can Native American culture survive in the white world?

Suggested Usage

Previewing Activities

- Students can research and locate on maps the Cheyenne and Sioux reservations in Montana, and in South and North Dakota.
- Teachers can have students research the American Indian Movement (AIM) and Wounded Knee, both of which are mentioned in the film.

Viewing Activities

GOOD PLACES TO STOP AND TALK

- After Philbert walks to the top of a sacred Indian mountain, he sees ribbons attached to branches of the trees. The teacher can stop the film here to discuss the cultural / spiritual significance of these ribbons.

PATTERNS/STRUCTURES TO LOOK FOR

- As the film is playing, the students can take notes for later discussion on how Buddy and Philbert differ and how Philbert changes Buddy.

Follow-up Activities

- Students can be asked to synthesize what they have learned of traditional and modern Native-American culture.
- Students can research Native Americans who live or have lived in the area they are now living in.
- Teachers can have students comment, orally or in writing, on what they think the film is saying about being a Native American today.
- Teachers can have students examine, orally or in writing, the stereotypes with which the film deals.

Other Considerations

None.

Ancillary Material

Churchill, Ward, and Jim Vander Wall. *Agents of Repression: The FBI's Secret Wars Against the Black Panther Party and the American Indian Movement.* Boston: South End Press, 1988.

Matthiessen, Peter. *In the Spirit of Crazy Horse.* New York: Viking Press. 1983.

Power

Subjects:	4, 22	**Director:**	Sidney Lumet
Playing Time:	111 minutes	**Producers:**	Reene Schisgal and Mark Tarlov
Rating:	R	**Date:**	1986
		Actors:	Richard Gere, Julie Christie, Kate Capshaw, Gene Hackman, Denzel Washington, E.G. Marshall, Beatrice Straight, Fritz Weaver

Plot Summary

A political consultant, Pete St. John, works for any candidate who has the money. One of his clients, Senator Hastings, whom he respects for his stand on solar energy, tells him he is not going to seek reelection because he is sick. Almost immediately St. John receives a call from a public relations man, Arnold Billings, who asks him to be the consultant for Cade, the man who will run for Senator Hastings' seat from the same party. Cade informs St. John that he agrees with Hastings' positions on all things except solar energy. St. John begins working for Cade, but he never really trusts him. Eventually he discovers, with the help of his ex-wife, a newspaper reporter, that Cade is working for foreign interests and that Arnold Billings had blackmailed Senator Hastings into retiring. And as a way of redeeming himself, St. John backs out of Cade's campaign.

General Commentary

This is a thought-provoking drama about how election campaigns are run in the United States. It touches on several important subjects: campaign commercials, smear campaigns, foreign lobbyists, personalized campaigns, and the entire campaign process itself. Anyone teaching about American politics would find this movie a useful resource.

Suggested Usage

Previewing Activities

- Teachers might have students research and report on what foreign and domestic lobbies are and how they can influence politicians.

- Teachers might also have students research and report on what Political Action Committees (PACs) are and what kind of influence they can have over an election. Teachers might also want students to research and report on laws and commissions that affect election campaigning in the United States: the Federal Election Campaign Act (FECA), the Federal Election Commission (FEC), and any state agencies and or laws (term limitation laws) that attempt to control election campaigning.

- Students can be asked to research and report on how election campaigns are conducted in England, where there is a limit put on the time spent campaigning, and compare that system with the U. S. system.

- Students can research and report on the decline of the influence of political parties in U.S. politics and the growth of the personalized campaign. To do this, teachers might want students to research the following kinds of topics: the historical role of political machines in this country, the growth of media in politics, the Kennedy-Nixon debate, and the growth of political consultants.

Viewing Activities

GOOD PLACES TO STOP AND TALK

- The second scene in the movie, in which St. John is giving advice to the man running for governor of New Mexico, is a useful one for ESL teachers to do a comprehension check. It sets up what St. John actually does for a living.

- The scene in which Arnold Billings is talking to the Arab oil sheik is critical for comprehension, particularly for ESL students, because it sets up the motivation of Billings and Cade.

- The scene in which St. John's ex-wife explains the business relationship she has discovered between Billings and Hastings' wife, and the subsequent scene where the wife explains how she got involved with Billings and what he forced her husband to do, are also critical. ESL teachers might want to stop and do a comprehension check after each of these scenes.

PATTERNS/STRUCTURES TO LOOK FOR

- ESL teachers can take advantage of many scenes to help students listen for inference. When St. John's ex-wife and business partner meet in the hotel lobby, much can be inferred about the type of relationship each had with St. John. The scene where St. John's former business partner comes to see him and asks for demographic information, and the scene directly after that where he is in bed with his assistant, can be used for inference activities with ESL students.

Follow-up Activities

- Students can research and report on a past campaign and discuss how it used commercials and print advertisements to create images of candidates. If you are teaching during an election period, you can use the current campaign.

- Students can be asked to come up with ideas of their own concerning election reform and present them in writing to their state or national representatives.

- Students can hold a formal or informal debate on the merits and demerits of the English and American election campaign systems.

- If you are teaching during a campaign period, students can examine and compare two opposing candidates' positions on campaign / election reform.

- Students can research and report on voter turnout in their state and area.

- ESL students can report on the election campaign / voting system in their countries.

Other Considerations

There are a shower scene and a couple of bedroom scenes.

The Razor's Edge

Subjects:	3, 14, 17, 19, 30	**Director:**	John Byrum
Playing Time:	129 minutes	**Producers:**	Robert P. Marcucci, Harry Benn, and Rob Cohen
Rating:	PG-13	**Date:**	1985
		Actors:	Bill Murray, Theresa Russell, Catherine Hicks, James Keach, Denholm Elliot

Plot Summary

Larry Darrell and Gray Maturin volunteer for the ambulance corps just prior to America's involvement in World War I. Idealistic Larry finds war horrifying. He watches his friends die, and he begins to wonder what life is all about. When he returns from war, his fiancee, Isabel, wants him to join a stock brokerage firm, get married, and settle down. Larry wants to find the answer to some questions. Larry begins his adventures to find the meaning of life in France and then travels "the razor's path" to Nepal. While Larry travels, Isabel can't wait for Larry to find himself and marries Gray. Ten years later they meet again in Paris. Larry has found himself (with a little help from a Hindu monk), and Gray and Isabel are recovering from the stock market crash. Larry eventually meets Sophie, an old friend, now an addict and prostitute. Larry helps Sophie recover and is about to marry her when she is brutally murdered by her old pimp. (Isabel is responsible for pushing Sophie over the edge.) Larry leaves for the United States an angry man.

General Commentary

This inferior remake of the famous 1946 film starring Tyrone Power has some interesting highlights and is Bill Murray's first dramatic role. The film can be used to study events during the early part of this century, the impact of the stock market crash, American ex-patriots, and the Somerset Maugham novel of the same name on which the film is based.

Suggested Usage

Previewing Activities

- Students can research the time period in which the film takes place and create a time line of events from 1917 to 1930.
- Teachers may encourage students to research drug addiction in Europe early in the 1900s.

Viewing Activities

GOOD PLACES TO STOP AND TALK

- Because the movie jumps back and forth from Larry to Gray and Isabel, it may help to stop the film at each character change to ensure that students understand what is happening.

- To help students understand the movie better, teachers may have students keep track of and describe the relationships between the friends and relatives in the film.

Follow-up Activities

- Students might research Upanishad scriptures and speculate why they inspired Larry to go to Nepal. Students can also do general research on Hinduism.

- The students may want to refer to their time lines from the previewing activity and see how many events the movie covered.

- Teachers might have students read the novel by Somerset Maugham and write a comparison paper.

- If possible, teachers can show the original movie and have students compare it with this remake.

- Teachers may want to have students research the stock market failure of 1929 (portrayed in the movie) and compare it to the stock market failure of 1989.

Other Considerations

The remake, although not as good as the original, does have better cinematography. Teachers are advised, if possible, to preview both the original and the remake.

Ancillary Material

Maugham, Somerset W. *The Razor's Edge*. New York: Doubleday, 1943.

The Razor's Edge. Directed by Edmund Goulding. 20th Century Fox, 1946.

A River Runs Through It

Subjects:	7, 10, 13, 17, 18, 24	**Director:**	Robert Redford
Playing Time:	124 minutes	**Producers:**	Robert Redford and Patrick Markey
Rating:	PG	**Date:**	1993
		Actors:	Craig Sheffer, Brad Pitt, Tom Skerritt

Plot Summary

This film centers on the relationship of two brothers, Paul and Norman Maclean, with each other and with their father. It is told through the eyes of the older brother Norman, the author of the book. Much of the narration is tied together by episodes in which the three men go fly fishing, from whence the title comes: a river running through a person's life. Set in Missoula, Montana, in the 1920s, the story moves chronologically from the boys' childhood, but most of the story focuses on the period of Norman's courtship of his wife, Jesse, and his gradual estrangement from his brother, a hard-living and hard-drinking newspaper reporter who is eventually killed in a fight because of his gambling. The movie shows how Norman and his Presbyterian minister father attempt to come to terms with this tragedy. Life, like the river, flows on.

General Commentary

This is a hauntingly beautiful, almost lyrical movie, that communicates more by what is felt than by what is shown or said. The story is simple and chronological, and the theme, of the "good" and the "bad" brother, is biblical in origin. There's no sex, no violence, and ideas and feelings are often expressed by little more than a look exchanged between two characters or a terse commentary by Norman, who narrates major portions of the movie. Because of the psychological depth of the movie and it's relative slowness, it would be best used with mature audiences who might be more capable of the psychological analysis this movie requires.

Suggested Use

Previewing Activities

- The students can read Norman Maclean's *A River Runs Through It* prior to watching the movie.
- If possible, a teacher could take students on a fishing trip. This movie is far more meaningful to students who have some background in fishing. Alternative activities would be to have local fishermen come in to tell about their hobby / occupation. Short readings from fishing magazines might also be useful.
- Depending on the composition of the class, the teacher could have students read up on famous disputes between brothers in history.

Viewing Activities

- For ESL purposes, their are many places where students can do paired viewings for description or narration, including the scene in which the brothers shoot the rapids and the scene in which Jesse drives down the railroad tracks.

- This is a movie about three male, white, Anglo-Saxon Protestants. Much of what makes this movie psychologically heavy is that so much is left unsaid and so much is implied. Almost any scene in which the two brothers interact as young men would be a good place to stop and have students discuss the questions: How does Norman / Paul feel and how do you know?

PATTERNS/STRUCTURES TO LOOK FOR

- A common theme is people coming to terms with behavior which they do not approve of or understand. The teacher can have students track the three main characters and discuss the answers to the following questions:

  What behavior does X disapprove of?

  Why do you think X disapproves of / does not understand this behavior?

  How does X show that he disapproves of / does not understand this behavior?

  How/why does X learn to tolerate this behavior?

Follow-up Activities

- In a related short clip at the end of the movie, there is a mini-documentary on what has happened to many western rivers. For an ecologically focused project, the teacher can have students research the history of the Blackfoot River featured in this movie.

- A teacher can assign additional readings on fishing, such as *The Old Man and the Sea* by Ernest Hemingway and certain passages from the Gospels (Mark 1:16–19). Fishing as a metaphor for the goal and purpose of life can be explored.

- A teacher can have students compare the book and the movie, which have enough differences to make such a comparison interesting.

- An ESL teacher can use this movie to spin off a variety of hypothetical speaking interactions. For example, in the movie there is a scene in which Norman and Paul have to deal with Jesse's brother, a man they obviously disapprove of. Students can develop roleplays in which they politely deal with rude people that they "have to" be nice to. In another scene, Norman must tell his father the bad news of Paul's death. Students could develop roleplays in which they practice telling someone something that is very unpleasant.

- It is possible to analyze these three men as representing one complete man: the father represents the spiritual side, Norman the emotional side, and Paul the physical side. Using these three divisions for analysis, a teacher can ask students to draw up a profile of white, Anglo-Saxon, Protestant men as portrayed in the movie.

Other Considerations

None.

Ancillary Material

Maclean, Norman. *A River Runs Through It, and Other Stories.* Chicago: University of Chicago Press, 1976.

The New English Bible. New York: Oxford University Press, 1972.

Hemingway, Ernest. *The Old Man and the Sea.* New York: Scribner, 1952.

Robin Hood: Prince of Thieves

Subjects:	1, 14, 16, 17	**Director:**	Kevin Reynolds
Playing Time:	138 minutes	**Producers:**	John Watson, Pen Densham, and Richard B. Lewis
Rating:	PG-13	**Date:**	1991
		Actors:	Kevin Costner, Morgan Freeman, Alan Rachman, Mary Elizabeth Mastrantonio

Plot Summary

This version of the legend of Robin Hood opens with Robin in an Arab prison during the Crusades. He escapes from prison with the help of a Moor named Azim. Robin and Azim return to England to find Robin Hood's father has been brutally murdered by the Sheriff of Nottingham, after the sheriff falsely accused him of devil worshipping. Robin is briefly reunited with Marian, a childhood friend and the sister of a fellow Crusader who died during the prison escape with Robin. Robin soon learns how the sheriff has ravaged the countryside and taxed people mercilessly to raise an army against King Richard the Lion-Hearted. Robin and Azim take refugee in Sherwood Forest from the sheriff who is hunting them. They join a community of poor peasants who are living off the land, and Robin Hood becomes their leader. The rest of the movie concerns how Robin brings down the sheriff and wins Marian's heart. Robin and Marian marry, and all live happily ever after.

General Commentary.

This is an excellent movie for all types of classes learning about legends. Because Robin Hood is a central legend in the West, it is an excellent film to use with ESL students.

Suggested Usage

Previewing Activities

- Teachers might have students research the Crusades, the reason why Robin was away from home when his father was murdered.

- Students can research the life of King Richard I of England (Richard the Lion-Hearted), who was the king when Robin Hood was supposed to have lived and who is critical to the story.

- Students can be asked to research what England was like in the 12th century (transportation, the church, leprosy, castle, sanitation, food, music and dance, costumes and clothing).

- ESL teachers might want students to read a version of the legend so they can become familiar with the story and characters (Little John, Friar Tuck, Maid Marian, the Sheriff of Nottingham, and Robin Hood).

Viewing Activities

GOOD PLACES TO STOP AND TALK

- The scene in which the sheriff's cousin reports to the sheriff about meeting Robin Hood, and the scene directly after that in which Robin Hood returns to his father's castle to find his father dead and meets the old blind servant, are important for understanding the story. ESL teachers might want to do comprehension checks after these two scenes.

PATTERNS/STRUCTURES TO LOOK FOR

- This version of *Robin Hood* attempts to bring a different perspective to the legend by having the Moor, Azim, present a contrast between the English (Western) world of the time and the Islamic (Eastern) world. Throughout the movie the viewer becomes aware of the differences in the two cultures and the advancements of the Islamic world (telescopes, cesarean births, explosives). A teacher might have students take note of these differences during the movie for discussion and further investigation afterward.

Follow-up Activities

- Since this version of Robin Hood attempts to break stereotypes (with a strong Maid Marian and the Moor, Azim) teachers might have students explore how this version has been updated by having them watch an earlier film version. Some critics criticized the movie for its changes, but this is a legend and doesn't have to follow historical fact.

- Students can investigate / research the theories that surround Robin Hood.

- Teachers can have students read Sir Walter Scott's 1819 *Ivanhoe*, in which the character of Locksley is Robin Hood.

- Teachers can have students research and report on the technological differences in the Eastern and Western worlds during the Middles Ages.

- ESL students can write on or do oral reports from their own culture about legendary characters who helped the poor or common people as Robin Hood did.

Other Considerations

None.

Ancillary Material

Miles, Bernard. *Robin Hood: His Life and Legend*. New York: Checkerboard Press, 1979.

Riley-Smith, Jonathan. *What Were the Crusades?*. London: Macmillan, 1977.

Scott, Walter. *Ivanhoe*. New York: Heritage Press, 1950.

Roxanne

Subjects:	9, 17, 25	**Director:**	Fred Schepisi
Playing Time:	107 minutes	**Producers:**	Michael Rachmil and Daniel Melnick
Rating:	PG	**Date:**	1987
		Actors:	Steve Martin, Shelley Duvall, Daryl Hannah, Michael Pollard, Rick Rossovich

Plot Summary

Charlie "C.D." Bales is the fire chief in a small town; Chris McDonell is a fireman who works for C.D., and Roxanne Kowalski is an astronomer visiting the small town for the summer. Roxanne is beautiful and intelligent. Chris is a moron and handsome. C.D. is intelligent and has a nose five inches long. C.D. loves Roxanne. Chris loves Roxanne. And Roxanne loves Chris's body and C.D.'s poetic verse, which she thinks is Chris'. The triangle becomes more complicated when Chris has to actually speak to Roxanne. Roxanne realizes that she loves the poetic voice of C.D. more than she could ever love Chris' body. The movie ends happily with C.D. and Roxanne getting together, and Chris finding a local waitress who loves him for what he is.

General Commentary

This great adaptation of Edmond Rostand's 1897 play, *Cyrano de Bergerac,* is a wonderful resource for anyone teaching the play, love and relationships, self-esteem, poetry, or drama.

Suggested Usage

Previewing Activities

- Teachers may want to have the students read *Cyrano de Bergerac* by Rostand.

- Two dramatic version of Cyrano de Bergerac are available on video. One, with José Ferrer, was made in 1950, and the other was released in 1990 and starred Gerard Depardieu. Teachers might want to show one of these videos prior to showing *Roxanne*

- Teachers might have students list, in order of importance, the qualities they think are important for a boyfriend / girlfriend or spouse to have.

Viewing Activities

GOOD PLACES TO STOP AND TALK

- Teachers may stop the film at the scene in which C.D. and Chris are talking to Roxanne from beneath the balcony. Students may be asked to compare this to the scenes from either the other films or the play itself.

- ESL teachers might want to do a reported and direct-speech activity involving the balcony scenes in the movie.

- Teachers may want their students to note the ways that C.D. deals with people staring at his large nose, such as the scene in which he makes up twenty better insults than the one given about his nose.

Follow-up Activities

- Secondary teachers may help students to become more aware and understanding of other people's handicaps by having their students visit and do an activity with special-needs students.

- Teachers might show the movie *Mask* and have the students note how the characters deal with their handicaps.

- Teachers might have students report on types of handicaps to make students more aware of the struggles others go through.

- Teachers can have their students compare and contrast the movie with the play or either of the two dramatic versions of the story on video.

- Teachers can have students write a comparison / contrast paper on C.D.'s and Chris' respective handicaps.

Other Considerations

Other than some occasional inoffensive profanity, there are none.

Ancillary Material

Morgan, Edwin, trans. *Edmund Rostand's Cyrano de Bergerac: A New Verse Translation.* Manchester: Carcanet, 1992.

Mask. Directed by Peter Bogdanovich. Universal Pictures, 1985.

Salvador

Subjects:	3, 14, 17, 22	**Director:**	Oliver Stone
Playing Time:	125 minutes	**Producers:**	Gerald Green and Oliver Stone
Rating:	R	**Date:**	1986
		Actors:	James Woods, James Belushi

Plot Summary

A freelance American journalist, Richard Boyle, travels to El Salvador in 1980 with Dr. Rock, a disc jockey friend. When they are not drinking heavily and smoking dope, Richard is reporting on the political events in El Salvador. His Salvadorian girlfriend's brother becomes a victim of a rightist death squad. Richard tries to trade information with two American intelligence officials in El Salvador to obtain official papers for his girlfriend, since without official papers she can be picked up by government forces at any time. They refuse to believe him when he tells them that the leftists have poor-quality weapons. Finally, Richard and John Cassady, another photojournalist, go into a battle zone where John is killed. Richard brings his girlfriend illegally over the Mexican-American boarder, only to have her arrested by U.S. immigration officials.

General Commentary

This is an excellent drama about what happened in El Salvador in the early 1980s, because it touches on just about every important event and issue during that period. For example, the movie deals with the assassination of Archbishop Oscar Romero, the killing of the Maryknoll nuns and lay worker, mysterious disappearances, the death squads, the influence of the Nicaraguan Sandinistas on the rebels in El Salvador, and the role of American aid and military intelligence officials in El Salvador. It is recommended for high school, ESL, or college-level students.

Suggested Usage

Previewing Activities

- Students can locate El Salvador and countries surrounding it on a map. If a road map is available, students can figure out how they could drive from the United States to El Salvador.

- Teachers might have students research the events that took place in El Salvador during 1980–1981. This will promote understanding of the many subplots and characters introduced in this movie.

- Students can research the history of El Salvador leading up to 1980.

- Teachers can have students read Joan Didion's book *Salvador*, which gives a very good description of life in El Salvador during this time.

Viewing Activities

GOOD PLACES TO STOP AND TALK

- Teachers might stop each time a significant character is introduced and have students focus on who the character is and what he/she represents or does. The following characters are important to the story: embassy officials, the ambassador, Mad Max, Mad Max's right-hand man, the human rights director, the Catholic lay worker, Archbishop Romero, the leftist commander, and the American intelligence officials. This will help ESL and secondary students, in particular, keep track of all the characters.

- After Richard and his John Cassady are in the dumping grounds for bodies, teachers might want to stop and discuss why and how many people disappeared in El Salvador.

PATTERNS/STRUCTURES TO LOOK FOR

- Richard is constantly giving Dr. Rock instructions on what to do and what not to do. Students can keep track of these scenes, since Dr. Rock's reactions are those of an average uninformed American about what was going on in El Salvador.

Follow-up Activities

- As Roger Ebert pointed out in his *Roger Ebert's Movie Home Companion 1990*, this movie's atmosphere owes a lot to Hunter Thompson, the author of *Fear and Loathing in Las Vegas*. Teachers can have students who have read this book compare elements of this book to parts of the movie.

- Teachers can have students bring in and share magazines and journals that have pictures of El Salvador taken in 1980–1981. These are examples of the types of pictures the photojournalists in this movie might have taken.

- Students can research what has happened in El Salvador since 1981 and what America's policy is toward El Salvador today.

- Students can match the characters in the movies to actual people who lived and worked in El Salvador at the time.

- Students can research further and report on the real Maryknoll massacre that was depicted in this film.

- Students can research and report on the human rights situation in El Salvador today. Amnesty International is an excellent resource.

Other Considerations

Be aware that there is a lot of violence and strong language and some nudity. ESL teachers should note that a lot of dialogue is difficult to understand because it is slurred or spoken very quickly. ESL teachers should note that the screenplay is available (see *Ancillary Material*).

Ancillary Material

Agee, Philip. *White Paper Whitewash: Interviews with Philip Agee on the CIA in El Salvador*. Ed. Walter Poelchau. New York: Deep Cover Books, 1981.

Americas Watch Committee: Lawyers Committee for International Human Rights. *Free Fire: A Report on Human Rights in El Salvador, August 1984* (Fifth Supplement.) New York: Americas Watch Committee, 1984.

Bonner, Raymond. *Weakness and Deceit: US Policy and El Salvador*. New York: Times Books, 1984.

Carrigan, Ana. *Salvador Witness: The Life and Calling of Jean Donovan*. New York: Simon & Schuster, 1984.

Didion, Joan. *Salvador*. New York: Simon & Schuster, 1982.

Erodozain, Placido. *Archbishop Romero, Martyr of Salvador*. Trans. John McFadden and Ruth Warner. New York: Orbis Books, 1981.

Forche, Carolyn. *El Salvador: Work of Thirty Photographers*. Eds. Harry Mattison, Susan Meiselas, and Fae Rubenstein. New York: W.W. Norton, 1983.

Stone, Oliver, and Richard Boyle. *Oliver Stone's Platoon and Salvador*. New York: Vintage Books, 1987.

Thompson, Hunter. *Fear and Loathing in Las Vegas: A Savage Journey into the Heart of the American Dream*. New York: Popular Library, 1971.

Serpico

Subjects:	4, 7, 11, 15	**Director:**	Sidney Lumet
Playing Time:	103 minutes	**Producer:**	Martin Bregman
Rating:	R	**Date:**	1973
		Actors:	Al Pacino, Tony Roberts

Plot Summary

This drama is based on the life of a real policeman who stood up against corruption in the New York City police force and found little support for his position. Frank Serpico is portrayed as a nonconformist who, on the surface, appears to have more in common with the criminal element than he does with other policemen. The film is as much a suspense drama as it is a cautionary tale of whistle-blowing and standing up for what you know is right.

General Commentary

This film was made in New York in the early 1970s, so some of what was contemporary then may seem strange to a younger audience. Yet it still works well with a high school, college, or high-level ESL audience exploring law enforcement, police corruption, whistle-blowing, or ethics.

Suggested Usage

Previewing Activities

- The teacher can have students research other famous whistle-blowing incidents (such as that of Karen Silkwood).

- The teacher can have students work through ethical-dilemma problems. For example: How far would you go to stop something you knew was wrong?

Viewing Activities

GOOD PLACES TO STOP AND TALK

- A major issue in the movie is the fact that no matter where Serpico works, he discovers corruption. ESL teachers might want to consider stopping the film each time Serpico is transferred to another precinct because transitions between jobs may be confusing for ESL students.

PATTERNS/STRUCTURES TO LOOK FOR

- Students can keep a list and description of each act of corruption and police brutality Serpico encounters.

Follow-up Activities

- Teachers might have students research the life of Frank Serpico by using New York newspapers that reported widely about the case.

- Teachers can have students do writing assignments on what they would have done had they been Frank Serpico. ESL teachers may want to review the unreal conditional with students before this writing assignment.
- Students can find newspapers and magazine accounts about other heros and then report to the class about these individuals. ESL students can do reports about heros from their own countries.
- Teachers can invite a real detective to class to speak about his/her work.
- Teachers can have students research and report on topics related to this film. These topics could include police brutality, corruption, rights of the accused, and crime.

Other Considerations

ESL teachers should be forewarned of the strong New York accents in the film. There is vulgarity, but it is realistically used.

Ancillary Material

Mass Peter. *Serpico*. New York: Vintage Press, 1973.

Glazer, Myron Peretz, and Penina Migdad Glazer. *The Whistleblowers: Exposing Corruption in Government and Industry*. New York: Basic Books, 1990.

Silkwood. Directed by Mike Nicholas. ABC Motion Pictures, 1983.

Silent Running

Subjects:	12, 18, 26	**Director:**	Douglas Trumbull
Playing Time:	90 minutes	**Producer:**	Michael Gruskoff
Rating:	G	**Date:**	1971
		Actors:	Bruce Dern, Cliff Potts

Plot Summary

The entire action of this movie takes place in 2008 on a space station several million miles away. Botanist Freeman Lowell (the name is no accident) tends the last plants in the universe under huge domes, and he longs for the beauty of a world that has disappeared. His shipmates point out that life on earth is wonderful: there may be no plants, but there is also no poverty and no unemployment. After eight years in space, command central tells the crew to destroy the domes and return to earth. Freeman is desperate to save the last beauty in the universe. He destroys the crew and directs the spaceship through the rings of Saturn, but command central finds him. In an attempt to save the last plants, Freeman sends the dome with the plants into distant space to be perpetually tended by a robot, then blows himself up.

General Commentary

This small, quiet film has a message that was ahead of its time and is still important today. The movie was made when environmental consciousness was just awakening, and it has a tendency to present choices in an either / or format: the economy or the environment, never both. Because the lines are clearly drawn, the film, properly presented, can be an excellent vehicle to spark discussion at all grade levels and also with ESL students.

Suggested Usage

Previewing Activities

- Younger students may benefit from a discussion of what life would be like without plants, and what role plants play in our ecosystem and climate.
- Students may report on environmental controversies, such as the spotted owl issue which pitted the preservation of endangered owls against the preservation of loggers' jobs.

Viewing Activities

GOOD PLACES TO STOP AND TALK

- ESL teachers might wish to check for comprehension after the scene in which Freeman discusses his view of life on earth with that of his shipmates.

- There is a lot of allusion to the situation on earth. Students can track what information is provided to develop a clear picture of life on earth. In addition, it's important for students to understand why Freeman wishes to preserve the trees; does he see them as necessary or simply as beautiful? Students can be asked to determine his feelings about the subject.

Follow-up Activities

- The teacher can lead a discussion in which students are asked to explain why they think the space station was put into space in the first place.

- Students can be asked to take a stand and defend a position on the central argument of the movie; which is more important, a healthy environment or a healthy economy?

- A binary presentation of the choices is presented: the economy vs. the environment. Students can do reports on eco-businesses to learn about how taking care of the environment makes good economic sense.

- Teachers might have students research and report on the Biosphere project.

Other Considerations

There is one scene of a choking.

Ancillary Material

Allen, John. *Biosphere 2: The Human Experiment.* Ed. Anthony Blake. New York: Viking, 1991.

Silkwood

Subjects:	3, 4, 7, 12, 15	**Director:**	Mike Nichols
Playing Time:	128 minutes	**Producers:**	Mike Nichols and Michael Hausman
Rating:	R	**Date:**	1983
		Actors:	Meryl Streep, Craig T. Nelson, Fred Ward, Kirk Russell, Diana Scarivid, Cher, Henderson Forsythe

Plot Summary

Karen Silkwood was a young worker at the Kerr-McGee plutonium plant in Oklahoma. A whistle-blower, she reported on numerous safety violations at the plant and became actively involved with the union. For her efforts, she became the target of a number of mysterious "contaminations." She died in a mysterious car crash on her way to deliver documents to a *New York Times* reporter. The movie tells this story, while presenting a view of her personal life and involvements with her boyfriend and roommate.

General Commentary

Karen Silkwood has been called America's first nuclear martyr, and after seeing this movie one can understand why. Contamination warnings always seems to be going off in the plant, and one wonders at the tenacity of people who continue to work there despite extremely sloppy and incredibly dangerous working conditions. It's an exciting and depressing movie, suitable for students in high school, college, or intermediate-advanced ESL courses.

Suggested Usage

Previewing Activities

- The teacher could have the students read Richard Rashke's *The Killing of Karen Silkwood*, on which the film is based.
- Students could research nuclear accidents and safety violations at nuclear power plants, including accidents at Hanford and Three Mile Island.

Viewing Activities

GOOD PLACES TO STOP AND TALK

- Several scenes are critical for comprehension, including the scenes of contamination, the union-organizing scene, and the scenes in which Karen gives information about the plant to reporters and union officials. Teachers would be well advised to do comprehension checks after these scenes.
- The scenes of contamination and the post-contamination process are excellent for reported / paired / mute narrations with ESL students.

- This story details a young woman's change in attitude about her job. Students can track those scenes in which Karen talks about her job to look for changes in that attitude.

Follow-up Activities

- Students can do library research about the settlement of Silkwood's estate.
- Students can do library research on local sources of nuclear energy, including those sources that might have had safety violations.

Other Considerations

There are a few bedroom scenes, although without sex or nudity.

Ancillary Material

Rashke, Richard. *The Killing of Karen Silkwood: The Story of the Kerr-McGee Plutonium Case.* Boston: Houghton Mifflin, 1981.

Glazer, Myron Peretz, and Penina Migdad Glazer. *The Whistleblowers: Exposing Corruption in Government and Industry.* New York: Basic Books, 1990.

Manuel, Cleo A. *Glowing on the Job: Worker Exposure to Radiation at Nuclear Power Plants.* 3rd. ed. Washington D.C.: Public Citizen Critical Mass Energy Project, 1990.

The Sting

Subjects: I, II
Playing Time: 129 minutes
Rating: PG

Director: George Roy Hill
Producers: Tony Bill and Mike and Julia Phillips
Date: 1973
Actors: Robert Redford, Robert Shaw, Paul Newman, Eileen Brennan

Plot Summary

This period piece is set in the Chicago underworld in the 1930s. Two small-time con artists team up to pull a major con on Doyle Lonegin, who controls the numbers rackets and was responsible for the death of a friend. Together they organize a variety of underworld types, all of whom share their loyalty to their dead friend, to pull a sting that involves horse racing reports via a tickertape. They succeed in getting Lonegin to bet a half-million dollars on the wrong horse, and the movie ends as they close down their sting operation.

General Commentary

This film sticks in the memory as a truly great movie. It has all the requirements for success: two likeable con artists played by Redford and Newman; a David-meets-Goliath plot, which quickly makes one forget that both David and Goliath are criminals; and a sense of the period, assisted in part by an authentic ragtime score, that few movies can imitate. It's not surprising this movie won a number of Oscars. It is appropriate for all audiences from mature junior high school through college. It should be noted, however, that this movie has what can only be called a "tricky" plot; there are a series of stings within the larger sting. It requires close attention and would be appropriate only for the most-advanced ESL students.

Suggested Usage

Previewing Activities

- Students could research and make presentations about the numbers racket as it was once managed by organized crime. In addition, some background reading on the history of organized crime in America, particularly on the non-Mafia organizations, would help students prepare to see this film. For example, a student-generated biography on the life of Dutch Schultz would be helpful, particularly since he is named in the movie.

- As either a previewing or postviewing activity, the teacher could play Scott Joplin's "The Entertainer" and present a little of the history of ragtime music.

- The teacher should preteach as much crime-related vocabulary as possible. As a minimum, the students should understand the title of the movie, the various meanings and forms of the word *con*, and the vocabulary of horse racing (*win, place, show, length, a head,* etc.). If there is a race track nearby, it should be possible to obtain dailies that can be turned into creative reading exercises with which to preteach this vocabulary.

Viewing Activities

GOOD PLACES TO STOP AND TALK

- The movie is conveniently divided into a number of "chapters" that are indicated by pages turning. It is an excellent idea to stop and check for comprehension after each chapter.

- As an absolute minimum, a teacher should stop and check for comprehension after the first scene in which Hooker and his pal con a numbers runner and after the scene on the train in which Gondorff "hooks" Lonegin. If students don't understand these two initial con jobs, they won't understand the point of the movie.

PATTERNS/STRUCTURES TO LOOK FOR

- This is a movie about a series of small con jobs leading up to one big con job. Teachers and students could track betting language throughout the movie.

- Each con job, from the very first to the last big one, has these common elements: a hook to appeal to the victim, a trap, and a getaway. Students can look for these common elements in the various con jobs they will see in the movie. Teachers can stop the tape after various small con jobs and see if students can identify the parts of the con job. About each con job, students should be able to tell who is tricking whom, and why.

Follow-up Activities

- Teachers can assign students to do reports on the lives of some of the famous gangsters of the early 20th century.

- Teachers can assign students to do a presentation on the life and music of Scott Joplin, whose music is featured in this movie.

- ESL teachers may find it interesting to discuss cross-cultural differences in organized crime.

Other Considerations

There are a few relatively non-sexual bedroom scenes. Again, teachers should be aware that the language of this movie is very slangy and requires careful, planned use.

Ancillary Material

Gammond, Peter. *Scott Joplin and the Ragtime Era*. New York: St. Martins Press, 1975.

Sann, Paul. *Kill the Dutchman! The Story of Dutch Schultz*. New Rochelle, N.Y.: Arlington House, 1971.

Talk Radio

Subject: 4
Playing Time: 110 minutes
Rating: R

Director: Oliver Stone
Producers: Edward R. Pressman and
A. Kitman Ho
Date: 1988
Actors: Eric Bogosian, Ellen Greene,
Leslie Hope, Alec Baldwin

Plot Summary

This is the story of talk radio host Barry Champlain, his rise to prominence, and his murder. The setting is Dallas, Texas, a fairly conservative city. Barry is a vociferous liberal Jew who loves to incite his listeners. His show is constantly "on the edge," and it goes overboard at some points. Throughout the show he expresses his liberal views and aggravates many of his listeners. By the end of the movie, he has received a number of death threats. Not taking them seriously, he leaves the station one night and is murdered as he walks to his car.

General Commentary

This is a great movie for many reasons. The number of subjects that can be addressed by teachers is almost unlimited. ESL teachers can use the dialogue of Barry and his listeners for a number of purposes. All teachers can use the film to help them talk about racism and other current issues. Finally, this movie can use the film in conjunction with the play *Talk Radio* by Eric Bogosian, or a host of other readings that were used to write the screen play.

Suggested Usage

Previewing Activities

• Teachers may have students research the rights and responsibilities of the press.

• Teachers may have their students research the Skinheads and other anti-Semitic groups.

• Teachers may have students research and report on the life of Alan Berg, a Denver talk radio host.

• Students can read the play of the same name by Eric Bogosian.

Viewing Activities

GOOD PLACES TO STOP AND TALK

• The scenes in which Barry is inciting his listeners are good places for the teacher to stop and discuss what Barry is doing, how he is doing it, and what the students think about what he doing.

• Scenes in which Barry insults his listeners are good places to stop and ask the students to think of reasons why he would do this and why listeners would not just turn off the radio.

- ESL teachers may have students read parts of the script before listening to the same scenes in the movie, since much of Barry's speech is rapid. ESL teachers can select scenes where Barry is insulting people. Students can discuss how Barry insults people.

PATTERNS/STRUCTURES TO LOOK FOR

- Teachers may want students to focus on Barry's relationship with different listeners. What makes the relationships unique?

Follow-up Activities

- Teachers might have students visit a talk radio station.

- Students may want to listen to a talk radio show and call in questions of their own.

- Teachers may want to invite a talk radio host to the class.

- ESL teachers may want students to listen to a national talk radio show host to discover what his/her point of view is (conservative, liberal, pro-Republican, pro-Democrat). ESL teachers may also want to have students do focused listening of radio advice shows. They are comparatively easy to understand and provide insight into the problems of many average Americans.

- Teachers can have students speculate, in writing or orally, why people call into talk radio shows and why people would continue to talk to someone who is insulting them.

Other Considerations

None other than occasional profanity.

Ancillary Material

Bogosian, Eric. *Talk Radio*. New York: Vintage Books, 1988.

Levin, Murray B. *Talk Radio and the American Dream*. Lexington, Mass.: Lexington Books, 1987.

Singular, Stephen. *Talked to Death: The Life and Murder of Alan Berg*. New York: Beech Tree Books, 1987.

Ten Little Indians

Subjects:	11, 17	**Director:**	George Pollock
Playing Time:	90 minutes	**Producer:**	Oliver A. Unger
	(black & white)	**Date:**	1966
Rating:	not rated	**Actors:**	Hugh O'Brian, Shirley Eaton, Stanley Holloway, Fabian, Wilfred Hyde-White

Plot Summary

Ten people are invited by a Mr. U.N. Owen (unknown) to a gathering at a remote mountaintop hideaway. Upon their arrival, a tape-recorded message informs them that each has been found guilty of a murder and then details the murders each is responsible for. An actress has killed her husband, a judge sentenced an innocent man, and a rock star ran over a couple while on a drinking binge, to name just a few of the crimes. When the horrified guests attempt to leave, they find themselves stranded, and one by one they die mysterious deaths. All this appears to be orchestrated to the progression suggested in the children's nursery rhyme "Ten Little Indians." Indeed, that poem is located in every room in the lodge, and a collection of porcelain figures of Indians is gradually disappearing. Finally, there is only one person left. . . .

General Commentary

This mystery is based on Agatha Christie's *And Then There Were None*. All the elements of a great whodunit are here: a remote location; a motley crew of characters; one or two identifiable characters, including a hunk and a beauty; and an intriguing *leitmotif*. The black and white adds to the suspense. This is a great film for people of all ages and language backgrounds.

Suggested Usage

Previewing Activities

- A teacher could have the students read the story by Agatha Christie, but in the interest of maintaining the suspense, students should not read the ending until they've seen the movie.

- A teacher could have the students read and discuss the poem. This would be especially helpful for ESL students who may not know this culturally loaded information.

Viewing Activities

GOOD PLACES TO STOP AND TALK

- For a general comprehension check, the teacher might stop the tape after the scene in which the tape recording explains to the guests why they have been assembled.

- It's an excellent idea to stop the tape after each murder and ask students to explain who they think might have "done it."

- After each murder, students should try to analyze how the death and the poem are connected. There are some observable patterns a teacher can check for, including the pattern that the murders seem to follow a public confession by the murdered. In other words, even though all the guests are accused of murder at the beginning of the film, they aren't actually killed until they admit to the charges against them.

Follow-up Activities

- The students can compare the book and the movie.

- The teacher can show an earlier version of this movie, *And Then There Were None*, or one of the two remakes of this movie, and compare versions.

- The teacher can show *Murder on the Orient Express* (in which there is one murdered person and twelve suspects) and have students compare the two movies.

- Prior to watching the denouement of the film, the students can do a creative writing assignment in which they explain who they think "did it" and why.

Other Considerations

None.

Ancillary Material

Christie, Agatha. *Ten Little Indians*. New York: Dodd Mead, 1978.

Murder on the Orient Express. Directed by Sidney Lumet. Paramount Pictures, 1974.

And Then There Were None. Directed by Rene Clair. Harry M. Popkin, 1945.

Thousand Pieces of Gold

		Director:	Nancy Kelly
Subjects:	3, 6, 7, 17, 25, 29, 31	**Producers:**	Kenji Yamamoto and Nancy Kelly
Playing Time:	105 minutes	**Date:**	1991
Rating:	PG-13	**Actors:**	Rosalind Chao, Chris Cooper

Plot Summary

This is the real-life story of Polly Bemis (née Lalu Nathoy), a young Chinese woman who, in 1880, is sold by her father and taken to the United States to her new owner, a Chinese saloon keeper in Idaho. On her way to Idaho, she falls in love with the Chinese tracker, Jim, who has been hired to take her to her owner. Because of her position as a slave, their love has no future. In Idaho she meets white and Chinese miners and American saloon keeper, Charlie Bemis, whose saloon is next to the one she works in. Charlie eventually wins her freedom in a poker game, but instead of living with Charlie, who really loves her, she opens a boarding house with his help. Eventually they do marry and move to a farm in the countryside.

General Commentary

This movie is adapted from Ruthanne Lum McCunn's book, *Thousand Pieces of Gold*. Those who have read the story will see that the movie is an interpretation of Polly Bemis' early life in the United States. It is an excellent movie for studying about the Chinese or Asian immigrant experience in the United States as well as about women in the old West.

Suggested Usage

Previewing Activities

- ESL, secondary, and college teachers can have students read Ruthanne Lum McCunn's novel.
- Students can research the Chinese incentive for coming to the United States.
- Students can research the lives of pioneer women in the old West.

Viewing Activities

GOOD PLACES TO STOP AND TALK

- Teachers might stop after the scene in which Charlie confronts an angry anti-Chinese group. From this point on, the movie focuses on the effects of the anti-Chinese movement on the local Chinese.

PATTERNS/STRUCTURES TO LOOK FOR

- Students can keep track of the types of people Polly meets in America. The different types of people reveal the different motivations for moving west: the miners from all over the United States; a freed black slave; a German prostitute who indentured herself to come to the United States; the Chinese miners; Hang King (the Chinese saloon keeper); and the Chinese herbalist.

Follow-up Activities

- Teachers can have students research the anti-Chinese movement and the Anti-Chinese Exclusion Act, both of which are referred to in the movie.

- Teachers can have students research the current wave of illegal Chinese coming to the United States and discuss the similarities and differences in Polly's situation.

- Students can compare the novel and the movie, which are very different.

- Students can research the experiences of other Asian immigrants.

- Students can research their local history to discover what types of pioneers / settlers came to their area.

- Students can research and report on the development of Chinatowns in the United States.

- Secondary students can research and report on the customs and traditions that surround the Chinese New Year.

- ESL students can write or report on what it was like for them when they first came to this country.

Activities for Low-Level ESL Students

The following activities are suggested for use with low-level ESL students. A teacher can:

- do a mute viewing of the scene in which Polly enters the town up until the time she kicks the rude man. Teachers may want students to write a dialogue for the scene and discuss how they think Polly might have felt.

- have students listen to and view the scene in which the African-American man buys a beer from Polly up until he says, "I'm going to tell you something you should know." Teachers can have students discuss what he might tell her. This is a critical scene because the conversation is not actually heard but its content is later alluded to.

- do a mute viewing with half the students of the scene in which Hang King ties Polly up and sells tickets to men who want to have sex with her up until Charlie wins her in the poker game. Students can then narrate the scene to a classmate who hasn't seen it. Then the students who didn't view it can listen to and view the entire scene. This group can then help the first group (who saw the mute viewing) revise their narrations. Last, all the students view the scene together for general comprehension. Teachers may also have students speculate on how Polly will feel about being won by Charlie and then compare it to how she actually feels once she is in Charlie's house in the following scene.

- have students do a mute viewing of the scene in which Jim returns to buy Polly's freedom until he leaves and she has a flashback of her father leaving her. Teachers can have students discuss what happens in the scene, why Jim leaves, why it reminded Polly of her father leaving her, and what she might do now.

- review with students the ways people give advice and make suggestions, and then have students listen to the scene in which Charlie goes to Hang King's window and gives him advice about leaving town. Students can be asked to write down what suggestions and advice Charlie gives to Hang King.

- have students view the scene in which the Chinese are leaving town and Polly has two conversations and gets very different advice from Li Dick and Hang King. Have students listen for what advice she receives and then for what advice she follows. Students can then be asked to discuss how Polly has changed.

Other Considerations

This movie was also released as an American Playhouse Drama on PBS; nevertheless, it should be available at your local video store. At the beginning of the movie the main female character has a strong accent; however, it in no way prevents comprehension. The first ten minutes of the movie contains English subtitles for the Chinese.

Ancillary Material

McCunn, Ruthanne Lum. *Thousand Pieces of Gold*. Boston: Beacon Press, 1981.

Elsensohn, M. Alfreda. *Idaho Chinese Lore*. Cottonwood: Idaho Corporation of Benedictine Sisters, 1979.

Elsensohn, M. Alfreda. *Idaho County's Most Romantic Character: Polly Bemis*. Cottonwood: Idaho Corporation of Benedictine Sisters, 1987.

Kitano, Harry, and Roger Daniels. *Asian Americans: Emerging Minorities*. Englewood Cliffs, N.J.: Prentice Hall, 1987.

Three Men and a Baby

Subjects:	9, 13, 25	**Director:**	Leonard Nimoy
Playing Time:	102 minutes	**Producers:**	Ted Field and Robert W. Cort
Rating:	PG	**Date:**	1987
		Actors:	Ted Danson, Steve Guttenberg, Tom Selleck

Plot Summary

Peter, Michael, and Jack live the charmed lives of carefree, totally uncommitted bachelors in a well-furnished penthouse overlooking Central Park in New York. Very little in the way of commitment concerns them until they find a baby girl on their doorstep. The baby turns out to be a product of one of Jack's flings. They were expecting the delivery of a package, but not one with a baby. As it turns out, the package they were expecting has heroin in it, but they weren't expecting that either! They spend the rest of the movie trapping the bad men who delivered the package with heroin and falling in love with the baby. The baby's mother comes back to claim her, but the guys can't give her up—so they invite the mother to live with them.

General Commentary

This delightfully silly comedy can be exploited in a number of ways by a creative teacher. It manages to poke fun at free love and sex, endorse parenthood, and put in a pitch against drugs—between some hilariously funny scenes and dialogue. It's one of a number of "saved by a baby" movies that have serious pedagogic potential.

Suggested Usage

Previewing Activities

- This movie is not hard to understand and needs little preteaching. However, a teacher may want students to view the original French comedy (available at larger video stores) for purposes of follow-up comparison.

- ESL teachers may wish to acquaint their students with the word "yuppie" and preteach a little about that word and about a profile of the type of person the word evokes.

Viewing Activities

GOOD PLACES TO STOP AND TALK

- ESL teachers may wish to exploit the following scenes for paired / mute / reported narrations:

  the opening scene in which the song "Boys Will Be Boys" is heard

  the scene in which Peter finds the baby

  the scene in which the three men trap the crooks with the heroin

  any of the scenes in which the three men integrate the baby into their lives

- The scenes pertaining to the initial drop off of the package of heroin might be a bit difficult for ESL students. There is a play on the word "shit" that a teacher may wish to stop and explain.

PATTERNS/STRUCTURES TO LOOK FOR

- An interesting pattern to look for is the way women are portrayed in this movie. A teacher may wish to assign students to look for the following female characters and to analyze those characters for their reaction to the baby and the situation: Peter's girlfriend, Rebecca; Michael's girlfriend; the landlady; Jack's mother; the women in the park; and Sylvia.

Follow-up Activities

- If the students have seen the French version of the film (highly recommended), a discussion of cross-cultural differences in humor can be held. The title of the French version is *3 Men and a Cradle*.

- Students may be guided to an analysis of what this movie says about the attitude of women toward children. Students can be asked to support their opinions with examples taken from the women in the film.

- If the students have seen another "parenting" movie (such as *Baby Boom*) they may be guided to an analysis of what this genre of film says about American values with respect to family and child-rearing.

Other Considerations

There is one bedroom scene, but no is sex shown.

Ancillary Material

3 Men and a Cradle. Directed by Coline Serreau. Samuel Goldwyn Company, 1986.

Tootsie

Subjects: 4, 9, 25, 27
Playing Time: 116 minutes
Rating: PG

Director: Sydney Pollack
Producer: Dick Richards
Date: 1982
Actors: Dustin Hoffman, Teri Garr, George Gaines, Jessica Lange, Bill Murray, Sydney Pollack

Plot Summary

A New York actor, Michael Dorsey, cannot find jobs because he is difficult to work with. Desperate, he dresses up as and pretends to be a woman to land a role in a soap opera. There he discovers what it is like to be treated like a woman, and in his case a not-so-attractive woman. He transforms his soap opera character from a weak to a strong person and, in the process, attracts a following of loyal fans. Meanwhile he becomes more and more attracted to the show's female lead, Julie, who is a friend. Eventually Michael, tired of hiding himself from Julie and wanting to escape from his contract, "comes out" in a hilarious live broadcast of the soap. Julie feels betrayed and angry at Michael but eventually forgives him for deceiving her, and they renew their friendship—this time as man and woman.

General Commentary

This is a very entertaining comedy about men and women and how they interact with each other. At the end of the movie, Michael realizes he is a better man for having been a woman. The main message is that men are often not all they can be, and neither are women. The movie is a useful resource for high school, ESL, or college-level students studying about stereotypes, sex roles, and relationships.

Suggested Usage

Previewing Activities

• Teachers might have students discuss stereotypes their culture/s has/have about women and men.

• Teachers might want to have students try to define in writing what they think it means to be a man and/or what it means to be a woman.

Viewing Activities

GOOD PLACES TO STOP AND TALK

• ESL teachers might want to stop in two places for comprehension checks: the opening scene which introduces Michael Dorsey and establishes he is an actor, and the scene in which Michael goes to his agent's office to find out why he hasn't gotten a part. Both scenes are critical for understanding who Michael is and why he felt desperate enough to dress up like a woman to get a job.

- Teachers might want students to keep track of and describe what they think Michael learns while he is Dorothy and what experiences he might never have had if he had not "been" Dorothy.

Follow-up Activities

- Students can write on or discuss how the experience of "being" Dorothy affected Michael's life.

- Since the movie touches upon the issue of sexual harassment (that of the director), teachers might want to have students research what sexual harassment is and what laws protect people against it.

- Another issue discussed in the movie is whether a powerful woman is threatening. Teachers can have students examine their own stereotypes of women and men by discussing what the concepts of femininity and masculinity mean to them.

- On a related topic, students can be asked to research and report on the acceptance of male actors playing female roles in other cultures and in the past.

- Students can compare this film to the recently released film *Mrs. Doubtfire*.

Other Considerations

None.

Topaz

Subjects:	1, 4, 8, 17	**Director:**	Alfred Hitchcock
Playing Time:	124 minutes	**Producer:**	Alfred Hitchcock
Rating:	PG	**Date:**	1970
		Actors:	Frederick Stafford, John Forsythe, John Vernon, Dany Robin, Karin Dor, Michel Piccoli

Plot Summary

A Soviet agent defects to the Americans somewhere in Scandinavia in 1962. Michael Nordstrom is the head of an intelligence agency that gets the first shot at debriefing the defector. The information given to Nordstrom points to a highly placed leak in NATO from within the French government. Nordstrom enlists the help of his French friend, André Devereaux, in finding the spy. Devereaux's inquiry leads him to Castro's Cuba, France, and New York City. Soviet missiles in Cuba and highly placed French spies are just some of the intrigue discovered. Eventually, Devereaux uncovers the name behind the leak, Topaz, and helps his American friend plug the leak. The Cold War continues with a few less spies.

General Commentary

This film can be helpful to teachers exploring the Cold War and the early sixties. In addition, teachers may find this movie appealing if students are reading the novel *Topaz* by Leon Uris. The plot is loosely based upon the "Sapphire" scandals, and the life of French spy Philippe de Vosjoli.

Suggested Usage

Previewing Activities

- Teachers may want students to look through microfilm of newspapers from the early sixties and find articles pertaining to the "Sapphire" scandals.
- Students might read the novel *The Missiles of October* to gain a background of what was happening at the time.

Viewing Activities

GOOD PLACES TO STOP AND TALK

- The teacher may have students stop at the scene in which André Devereaux decides to help his American friend, Michael Nordstrom. What is Devereaux's motivation? Why is he willing to risk so much to help his friend?

PATTERNS/STRUCTURES TO LOOK FOR

- Teachers might have the students look for and note stereotypes of Russians and Cubans.

- Teachers might point out a bit of film history trivia. Hitchcock always appears briefly in every movie he made. Show the class his picture and have them look for him in the film.

Follow-up Activities

- The teacher may have the students research and report on why the French spies did what they did.
- The teacher may have the students write an editorial on the Topaz ring from a French point of view.
- Teachers might have students explore the Cold War. What did it mean then? What does it mean now?
- Teachers can have students write about what stereotypes of Russians and Cubans are presented in the film.
- Teachers can have students read the book of the same name and compare it to the movie.

Other Considerations

None.

Ancillary Material

Uris, Leon. *Topaz*. New York: McGraw-Hill, 1967.

Thompson, Robert Smith. *The Missiles of October: The Declassified Story of John Kennedy and the Cuban Missile Crisis*. New York: Simon & Schuster, 1992.

Trading Places

Subjects:	4, 9, 17, 23	**Director:**	John Landis
Playing Time:	106 minutes	**Producer:**	Aaron Russo
Rating:	R	**Date:**	1983
		Actors:	Dan Ackroyd, Eddie Murphy, Ralph Bellamy, Don Ameche, Jamie Lee Curtis

Plot Summary

Louis Winthrop III and Billy Ray Valentine are extreme opposites—culturally, socially, and economically. To resolve a bet, Winthrop's rich and eccentric bosses, who are brothers, contrive to have Winthrop and Billy Ray switch positions. Street hustler Billy Ray is transformed into high-powered yuppie executive, and Winthrop finds himself in Billy Ray's shoes. Eventually Billy Ray and Winthrop work together to bring down the rich brothers who forced them to trade places. Although the film is a comedy, there is a bigger message hidden in the slapstick antics of the story.

General Commentary

This is a genuinely funny film, but the plot has been used many times. English teachers would find Mark Twain's *The Prince and the Pauper* an appropriate reading prior to watching the film. Other teachers may want to use the film for its economic message and the question it raises about heredity versus environment. Teachers will also find the stereotyping in the film to be a resource for multicultural education.

Suggested Usage

Previewing Activities

- Teachers may have the students read *The Prince and the Pauper* by Mark Twain.
- Teachers might want students to study the issues of the homeless.
- Teacher can also have students discuss whether they think heredity or environment determines success.

Viewing Activities

GOOD PLACES TO STOP AND TALK

- The teacher may want to stop the film immediately after Louis and Billy Ray switch roles so students can speculate on who will fare better in his new role.
- ESL teachers might stop the movie for a comprehension check right after the brothers reveal why they have made the bet because knowing that the brothers had a bad motive turns the direction of the viewers' opinion of the story. Teachers can have students discuss what the revelation reveals about how the brothers look at other people.

- Teachers can have students keep track of what Louis and Billy learn about the world and themselves by walking in each others' shoes.

Follow-up Activities

- The teacher may want to discuss what racist attitudes are portrayed in the movie.

- Teachers may want the students to research and report on the demographics of the superrich and the very poor in the United States.

- Teachers may have the students play the Stock Market game to get a feeling for the vast amount of money that can be made or lost in playing the "market."

- The teacher may want to invite a commodities broker to the classroom to explain what he/she does.

- Students can write about how Louis and Billy changed by having lived each others' lives.

- Students can be given a creative-writing assignment, such as selecting two people they would most like to see trade places (world leaders, famous historical people, etc.), then explaining why they selected the two people and how each might (have) change(d) from the experience. ESL teachers may want to review unreal future and past conditionals with students before making this assignment.

Other Considerations

There is some profanity, and a few scenes show prostitution.

Ancillary Material

Mark Twain. *The Prince and the Pauper: A Tale for Young People of All Ages.* New York: Nelson Doubleday, 1970.

12 Angry Men

Subjects:	4, 15, 23	**Director:**	Sidney Lumet
Playing Time:	93 minutes	**Producers:**	Henry Fonda and Reginald Rose
Rating:	not rated	**Date:**	1957
		Actors:	Henry Fonda, Lee J. Cobb, Ed Begley, Jack Warden, Martin Balsam, Jack Klugman

Plot Summary

This drama takes place in a jury room where twelve men are deliberating the fate of a young (perhaps Puerto Rican) man accused of murdering his father. The story shows how the jury comes to its decision to find the young man not guilty. The movie portrays the different motivations of each juror, the prejudices of several of the jury members, and one juror's positive influence over the deliberating process.

General Commentary

This is an excellent movie for teaching several different topics. Because the movie is based on the real-life experience of the screenwriter, Reginald Rose, while sitting on a jury, the movie is probably the most authentic representation of a jury deliberation on film. Therefore, teachers teaching about the American legal system might find this a useful resource. Further, because the movie deals forcefully with the issue of prejudice and racism, it is an excellent resource for teaching about bias, prejudice, and racism. Last, the movie portrays an individual standing up against a group to defend an idea and a principle he believes in. For that reason the movie is classic in its appeal.

Suggested Usage

Previewing Activities

- Teachers may want students to research and report on the jury system in their state. ESL teachers may want to preteach the following vocabulary: *sequester, foreman, court-appointed lawyer, evidence, witnesses,* and *hung jury.*

- Teachers may arrange for students to visit a courtroom and listen to a jury trial, then do a mock deliberation of their own on the case and compare it with the actual jury's decision.

- If possible, teachers may invite a judge to speak with the students about the role of the jury. This could be included in a larger activity, such as a tour of a courthouse.

- Students might benefit from a discussion on what "reasonable doubt" means, since it is critical to the action of this drama.

- Students can discuss examples of how individuals can change the way a group thinks. If students are unable to think of examples the movie presents an excellent one.

Viewing Activities

GOOD PLACES TO STOP AND TALK

- ESL teachers may want to do a comprehension check right after the judge gives his instructions to the jury, which sets up the rest of the action. If students don't understand the consequences of a guilty verdict (the boy will be sent to the electric chair), the rest of what goes on will not have the same impact.

- Teachers may want to stop after each vote to have students discuss who changes their vote and why.

PATTERNS/STRUCTURES TO LOOK FOR

- The racism and prejudice some of the jury members feel toward the defendant is seen in their language (for example, referring to "those kinds of people"). Teachers may want to have students write down the different ways racism is portrayed.

- The one very obvious pattern in this movie relates to the different types of people on the jury. Teachers may want students to keep track of the physical and behavioral characteristics of each juror in order to do a character analysis after the film. In classes of at least twelve students, each student can keep track of just one character on the jury.

- Teachers can have students keep track of the evidence against the defendant and the counter-evidence that was provided during the jury deliberation.

Follow-up Activities

- Teachers may want students to write physical and behavioral descriptions of each character. One way of doing this is for teachers to give students questions about each of the characters, for example:

  What motivated each of the characters?

  Why did each member change his vote?

  How did each member interact with the other members?

- Teachers may want students to compare and contrast one juror with another juror.

- Teachers can have students discuss and/or write about what evidence was used against the boy and what counter-evidence was provided during the jury deliberation.

- Teachers may want students to research and report on controversial jury verdicts (such as the first L. A. policemen's trial in the Rodney King beating, the 1993 Randy Weaver trial in Idaho, and the 1993 Reginald Denny beating trial).

- Teachers can also follow up by having students view the documentary film *A Thin Blue Line* (1988), which documents the case of a man who was wrongly convicted of the murder of a Dallas police officer and spent thirteen years on death row.

- Teachers may have students discuss what it means to be judged by a jury of one's peers. For example, in the film the jury was made up completely of men, most of whom were white.

- If possible, teachers may invite to class a person who has been on a jury to discuss his/her experience.

- Teachers may want to have students discuss and/or write about what Henry Fonda's character (the man who stood up against the group) might symbolize (for example, the individual making a difference). ESL teachers may want students to discuss what they think the film was saying about Americans and American society.

- Teachers might have students follow up by researching and reporting on the history and development of the jury system in the West and specifically in America. ESL teachers may want students to compare the American system with the ones in their countries and examine how the differences in the systems reflect underlying cultural differences.

Other Considerations

None.

Ancillary Material

The Thin Blue Line. Directed by Errol Morris. Miramax, 1988.

The War of the Roses

Subjects:	4, 9, 27	**Director:**	Danny De Vito
Playing Time:	116 minutes	**Producer:**	James L. Brooks
Rating:	R	**Date:**	1989
		Actors:	Michael Douglas, Kathleen Turner, Danny De Vito

Plot Summary

This black comedy, told in flashback by a divorce lawyer, tells the story of the meeting, marriage, divorce, and deaths of the Roses—a couple who play by the "take no prisoners" school of divorce. The story starts with their meeting and progresses to show how he developed into a lawyer obsessed with his job and she into a housewife obsessed with her home. When the kids move off to school, she decides to start her own catering business. Soon she's totally disenchanted with her marriage and asks for a divorce. As the divorce progresses, it becomes clear that neither partner will relinquish the house. Soon there's a war on, and the two feuding Roses do crueler and crueler things to get the other to give in and hand over the house. Eventually, they literally kill each other.

General Commentary

This would be an ideal movie to show in a high school family life class or in any class in which students undertake an examination of American family values. Its usefulness lies in the fact that the Roses are so recognizable and in many ways so enviable. They are bright, talented, attractive, rich people, who have a beautiful, healthy family and a home to be proud of. Yet they are an emotionally retarded couple who start growing apart on their first date. That they get divorced is no surprise. What is surprising is the passion with which they struggle for their home. And the moral of the story lies in the horror as the struggle unfolds and as the lawyer's voice explains what went wrong.

Suggested Usage

Previewing Activities

- Depending on the class, the teacher could lead a discussion on what is really important for a person to get out of a divorce. This could be used as a values-clarification exercise in a psychology or family life class.

- The students could do some very basic research about the historical significance of the title (the Tudor / and Stuart War of the Roses) and predict what the movie might be about.

Viewing Activities

GOOD PLACES TO STOP AND TALK

- The teacher may stop the video after the lawyer's opening remarks to have students predict what the rest of the story will be about.

- Scenes that are critical to comprehension are few, but the scene in which the lawyer tells Oliver Rose that he has the legal right to stay in the house is a good one to make sure that students understand.

PATTERNS/STRUCTURES TO LOOK FOR

- The Roses' relationship is told in a series of flashbacks, and the teacher can stop the tape after each scene so students can examine the scene for signs of trouble in the relationship.

Follow-up Activities

- An exciting, values-clarifying ESL-appropriate speaking activity can be developed by stopping the tape before the final scene in which the Roses kill each other. The "rest of the story" can be roleplayed / debated by students in an attempt to determine who should get the house.

- As a creative writing assignment, students can write an obituary for the Roses.

- More mature students can research their state laws to find out what would happen to the house in their state.

Other Considerations

There are one "bump-and-grind" sex scene, a few other bedroom scenes, and discussions of such topics as being multiorgasmic.

War Games

Subjects:	1, 8, 18	**Director:**	John Badham
Playing Time:	110 minutes	**Producer:**	Harold Schneider
Rating:	PG	**Date:**	1983
		Actors:	Matthew Broderick, John Lithgow, Ally Sheedy, Dabney Coleman, Barry Corbin

Plot Summary

David is a computer whiz in his final year of high school. While trying to impress a young lady, Jennifer, he accidentally hacks his way into a computer at the Department of Defense. He chooses a game on the computer called "Global Thermonuclear Warfare." Immediately, the United States goes on full alert and the Soviet Union responds accordingly. Realizing this was not what he had in mind, David goes searching for ways to call the game off. He and Jennifer spend the rest of the movie trying to stop the game from causing World War III. Finally as things look hopeless, they find a very simple answer for what may have been a "final solution."

General Commentary

This drama / thriller dredges up memories of the Cold War and that in itself makes the film very useful. Teachers may find the film useful when discussing the idea of *brinksmanship* and other concepts that are a part of the Cold War vocabulary. In addition this film may also be used to discuss computers and hacking, which can lead to discussions of high-tech espionage and terrorism.

Suggested Usage

Previewing Activities

- Teachers may have the students research the Cold War.

- Teachers may want students to find out what *global thermonuclear warfare* means.

- Teachers may have students report on the military build-up in the United States during the 1970s and 1980s. Teachers can have students research the theory of Mutual Assured Destruction (MAD), which was the basis of America's nuclear strategy and which is central to understanding parts of this film.

- Teachers might bring in a modem and show students how to access information over the phone lines.

- Teachers can discuss metaphor and have students compile a list of metaphors that describe things they know. The following are some examples: time is money; war is hell; life is a stage and we are actors; and war is business.

Viewing Activities

- ESL teachers may want to stop the film to do a comprehension check after David breaks into the high school computer, since the scene sets up the fact that David has the ability to hack into computers.

PATTERNS/STRUCTURES TO LOOK FOR

- Students can look for the metaphors in this movie: war is a type of game, Global Thermonuclear Warfare is tic-tac-toe.

Follow-up Activities

- Students can discuss how war is like a game (For example: it has two sides, it is a competition, it has rules, it has winners and losers, etc.). Further, students can discuss how Global Thermonuclear War is like a game of tic-tac-toe. This is a useful exercise for helping students see how metaphor has an internal logic that extends into a comprehensive perspective on a subject.

- Students can research and report on hacking incidents, using the following questions:

    Who were the hackers?

    What computers did they hack into?

    How did they get caught?

    What happened to the hackers?

- Teachers may want students to learn how to use a modem to access information legally.

- Teachers might have the students watch earlier films, such as *Fail Safe* or *Dr. Strangelove*, and compare their messages to the message in *War Games*.

- Students may be asked to define *brinksmanship* as a political term. They then can research times when that philosophy was practiced as a policy of our government (the Cuban Missile Crisis).

- Students can be asked to think of other Cold War metaphors (For example: the Soviet Union is an evil Empire; the Chinese were a red horde). Teachers can have students discuss how these metaphors shape the collective reality of Americans and how political leaders use(d) them to advance their political aims (such as Ronald Reagan's use of the "evil empire" metaphor to build up America's nuclear arsenal).

- Students can research and report on what is happening with America's nuclear weapons now that the Cold War is over.

- Teachers can also have students discuss and debate the question of whether scientists have a moral responsibility to ensure that their discoveries and inventions are used ethically.

Other Considerations

None.

Ancillary Material

Allen, Thomas B. *War Games: The Secret World of Creators, Players and Policy Makers Rehearsing World War III Today*. New York: McGraw-Hill Book Company, 1987.

Dr. Strangelove: Or How I Learned to Stop Worrying and Love the Bomb. Directed by Stanley Kubrick. Columbia Pictures, 1963.

Fail Safe. Directed by Sidney Lumet. Columbia Pictures, 1964.

Wilson, Andrew. *The Bomb and the Computer: Wargaming from Ancient Chinese Mapboard to Atomic Computer*. New York: Delacorte Press, 1968.

Where the River Runs Black

Subjects:	10, 12, 18, 24	**Director:**	Chris Cain
Playing Time:	100 minutes	**Producers:**	Joe Roth and Harry Ufland
Rating:	PG	**Date:**	1986
		Actors:	Charles Durning, Alessandro Rabelo

Plot Summary

A priest begs another priest for forgiveness of a sin, which he relates in a long flashback. A boy (Lazaro) and a priest live together near the city of Manaus, Brazil. The boy's parents were a beautiful, mysterious, Indian dolphin-woman and a young Catholic priest who died shortly after the boy was conceived. Lazaro and his mother live by themselves upstream in a sort of jungle idyll until gold prospectors kill the mother. The boy is caught by dolphin-poachers and brought to Manaus, where he is befriended by the priest friend of his father's and sent to a Catholic school. One of the gold prospectors who killed Lazaro's mother, now a politician running for governor of the state, visits the school, where Lazaro recognizes him as his mother's killer. Lazaro and a friend follow the man and attempt to kill him. The friend is caught and forced to work as a slave laborer in the politician's mines. Lazaro frees his friend and they return to the jungle together. The priest comes looking for them and, realizing it was wrong to take Lazaro from his jungle home, leaves him there, where "the river runs black" (the Rio Negro). But the politician shows up to kill the child who had witnessed his crime, and the priest kills him. This is the sin for which the priest begs forgiveness.

General Commentary

This beautiful, mysterious movie makes the viewer realize how terrible the destruction of the Brazilian rainforest has been to its inhabitants. The boy is a symbol of the indigenous peoples and of the forest itself, and the message seems to be that the only incursions that will succeed are those that become part of the forest itself. Catholicism will succeed if it blends and becomes part of and supportive of the culture, and all "top-down" incursions will be eradicated. The film can be used with high school, college, or ESL students. Although made in Brazil with mostly Brazilian actors, the spoken language is English.

Suggested Usage

Previewing Activities

- Without some idea of the region and the regional politics, the students would find this movie hard to understand. A teacher might want to start with a map-reading exercise to familiarize students with the area referred to in the movie.

- The movie touches on the gold mining that is now cutting into the lands of the Indians. Students might do library research to learn more about the politics of the region.

- Native Brazilian culture has many dolphin stories, stories which are roughly equivalent to Western Europe's mermaid stories. Students may be directed to read one of these stories before watching the film, which frames the story of the appearance of Lazaro's mother.
- A common understanding of Catholicism runs through this movie: priestly celibacy, confession, and biblical references to "the light on the waters." Teachers may wish to discuss some of these ideas with their students prior to watching the movie. This would be of particular use to ESL students from non-Catholic cultures.

Viewing Activities

GOOD PLACES TO STOP AND TALK

- There are several good places where ESL teachers can do mute / paired / reported narrations. These places include the following:

    the scene in which Lazaro's father first sees Lazaro's mother in the water

    the scene in which Lazaro's mother is killed

    the scene in which Lazaro is trapped and caught

    the scene in which Lazaro is brought to the school

    the scene in which Lazaro cleans the kitchen in the school

    the final scene in which the politician is killed

PATTERNS/STRUCTURES TO LOOK FOR

- From the very beginning of the movie, when the priest confesses his complicity in killing the politician, there is a tension between the concepts of action and inaction. There is a very Christian message that one should forgive one's enemies.

Follow-up Activities

- Students may be directed to do in-depth research on the plight of Brazil's Indians, in particular the Yanonami, and report either in writing or orally. This movie takes a very romantic view of the lifestyles of those Indians who have not had contact with Europeans. Students may wish to find out how true to life this depiction of the lifestyle is.
- As an extension of this activity, teachers may have students investigate the plight of North American tribes who have been victimized by prospectors in the search for mineral rights. The Sioux and their fight to keep their Black Hills from gold prospectors make an excellent North American parallel.
- Teachers may wish to have students read Hudson's *Green Mansions* to analyze another romanticization of the area discussed in this movie.
- Teachers may wish to have students discuss / decide whether what the priest did to the politician was wrong.

Other Considerations

There is a little brief, native-style nudity and a scene of implied sexual activity between a priest and a native woman.

Ancillary Material

Glueck, Nelson. *Deities and Dolphins*. New York: Farrar, Straus & Giroux, 1965.

Hudson, William Henry. *Green Mansions*. New York: Harper & Brothers, 1951.

White Fang

Subjects:	1, 10, 17, 29, 31	**Director:**	Randal Kleiser
Playing Time:	109 minutes	**Producer:**	Marykay Powell
Rating:	PG	**Date:**	1991
		Actors:	Ethan Hawke, Klaus Maria Brandauer

Plot Summary

This movie is based on the novel of the same name by Jack London. A young man, Jack, goes to the Yukon to work his dead father's mining claim. Jack, at first unwillingly, is helped to find the claim and is taught how to mine by one of his father's friends. A friendship grows between the two men. A more important aspect of the story is the friendship that develops between Jack and a half-wolf dog called White Fang. The movie ends with Jack and his father's friend discovering gold. When his father's friend moves to San Francisco to start a hotel, Jack remains in Alaska to continue mining and is emotionally reunited with White Fang.

General Commentary

This movie will appeal to students who enjoy adventure stories where an animal is the hero. It is also an excellent movie for students studying the Alaskan gold rush. Since the movie is very visual and the story is easy to understand, it is particularly useful for ESL students.

Suggested Usage

Previewing Activities

- Teachers can have students research and report on the Alaskan gold rush.
- Students can locate the Klondike and other areas discussed in the movie on a map.
- Students can research and report on the life of Jack London.
- Students can read the novel *White Fang*.

Viewing Activities

GOOD PLACES TO STOP AND TALK

- The opening scene until Jack finds his father's old friend who agrees to take him part of the way to his father's claim sets up the whole story. ESL students can identify the characters who are introduced and discuss what they have learned about the background and the motivation of the main character, Jack.
- Some of the scenes, mostly of animals in the wild, in which there is little or no dialogue can be used by ESL teachers for paired narration activities.

Viewing Activities

- Students can list the types of people who came to or who were native to Alaska, according to the movie (Native Americans, miners, gamblers, criminals, women entrepreneurs, and a Chinese gold specialist).

Follow-up Activities

- Teachers can have students read the Jack London short story "To Build a Fire," which relates well to the scene in this movie in which Jack's father's friend must build a fire to keep Jack warm.
- Students may read Robert Service's poem "The Cremation of Sam McGee," which also is very relevant to the movie.
- Students can compare the movie with the novel.
- Students can research the Native American tribes in Alaska and their philosophies / beliefs toward animals. Students can then compare those philosophies / beliefs with their own culture's philosophies / beliefs.

Activities for Low-Level ESL Students

The following activities are suggested for use with low-level ESL students: A teacher can:

- have students do a mute viewing of the scene in which Jack gets off the boat and meets the three villains. Students can look at body language and guess what is going on in the scene (the three men pick Jack's pocket). Then students can discuss the scene and answer questions. For example: Are the three men good or bad, and how do you know?
- have students do a mute viewing of the scene of the sled accident up until Jack's books are used to start a fire. Then have students do a narration activity based on what they saw.
- have students read the poem "The Cremation of Sam McGee," after Alex buries the body he has been hauling, and discuss why men went to the Yukon, what their lives were like there, what they missed, and why they stayed.
- have students listen carefully, perhaps with a cloze exercise, to the Indian chief's explanation of his attitude toward animals and specifically toward White Fang. Students can then discuss the role of animals and pets in their countries and cultures. If students have pets, encourage them to bring in pictures of the pets or describe them to the class.
- have half the class view the scene in which Jack and Alex rebuild the mine and then describe how the mine looks to classmates who have not seen the scene. Have the students who did not view the scene draw pictures of the descriptions they heard and compare them to each other's and then the actual mine in the movie.
- have students do a prediction exercise after Alex tells Jack he can't bring White Fang to San Francisco. Students can speculate as to what Jack will do and what they (the students) would do if they were Jack.

Other Considerations

None.

Ancillary Material

London, Jack. *White Fang*. New York: Scholastic Book Service, 1971.

London, Jack. *Short Stories of Jack London*. Edited by Earl Labor, Robert C. Leitz, III, and Milo I. Shepard. New York: Macmillan, 1990.

Service, Robert. *Dan McGrew, Sam McGee, and Other Great Service*. Dallas: Taylor Publishing Company, 1987.

White Nights

Subjects: 1, 8, 15, 23
Playing Time: 135 minutes
Rating: PG-13

Director: Taylor Hackford
Producers: Taylor Hackford and William S. Gilmore
Date: 1985
Actors: Mikhail Baryshnikov, Gregory Hines, Isabella Rosellini

Plot Summary

A Soviet dancer who defected from the U.S.S.R. finds himself back in the U.S.S.R. after the plane he is on crashes inside its borders. He is captured by the Soviet government and brought to live with Raymond, an African-American dancer who defected to the Soviet Union and is now living with his Russian wife in Siberia. The American, however, has grown dissatisfied with his life in the Soviet Union. The three decide to escape, and the film builds great suspense as it follows their efforts.

General Commentary

This is an unexceptional but enjoyable film. The secondary plot of the defected African-American and the outstanding dancing are its most interesting aspects. It is recommended for ESL and secondary teachers.

Suggested Usage

Previewing Activities

- ESL and secondary teachers might want to have students look up the word *defect*.
- Students might locate Siberia and Leningrad (now St. Petersburg) on a map.

Viewing Activities

GOOD PLACES TO STOP AND TALK

- ESL teachers might stop after the scene in which the American Ambassador explains why he won't second-guess the Soviet explanation of why they can't release the former Soviet dancer to the Americans. This scene explains why the American Embassy does nothing.

- The scene in which Raymond explains what motivated him to defect is full of implication. Raymond uses dance and words to communicate his feelings about racism in the United States and the Vietnam War. ESL and secondary teachers might want to have students listen critically for the implication in this scene.

PATTERNS/STRUCTURES TO LOOK FOR

- Have students look for stereotypes and images of Soviets (such as when the Soviet official takes Raymond to a construction site where the workers look like ants in an anthill).

- Have students keep track of how Raymond comes to realize that he is being used by the Soviet officials and that they don't really care about him.

Follow-up Activities

- Students can research and report on other Americans who defected to the former Soviet Union.

- Teachers can have students research and report on African-American artists who have left the United States for social, political, or artistic reasons (for example, Josephine Baker).

Other Considerations

None.

Ancillary Material

Rose, Phyllis. *Jazz Cleopatra: Josephine Baker in Her Time.* New York: Doubleday, 1989.

Witness

Subjects:	4, 11, 13, 18, 24, 31	**Director:**	Peter Weir
Playing Time:	112 minutes	**Producer:**	Edward Feldman
Rating:	R	**Date:**	1985
		Actors:	Harrison Ford, Lucas Haas, Patti LuPone, Kelly McGillis, Danny Glover

Plot Summary

This romantic thriller set in Lancaster County, Pennsylvania, begins with the murder of an undercover cop in a restroom in a Philadelphia train station. The only witness is a young Amish boy, Samuel Lapp, who soon identifies the killer as another cop (Danny Glover). Concerned for Samuel's safety at the hands of this corrupt cop, the detective investigating the murder, John Book, takes the child and his mother back to their farm in Lancaster and hides out there while trying to decide how to deal with the corrupt cop. On the farm Book "witnesses" the Amish lifestyle and falls in love with Samuel's mother, Rachel. The final showdown resolves both dilemmas.

General Commentary

This is a beautiful, highly visual, spine-tingling suspense movie, with the quirky twist that the action happens in a peaceful community that abhors the use of guns and violence. It's also a romance in the old-fashioned sense of the word, and it's hard to imagine any group of students who would not find something to enjoy in viewing the film.

Suggested Usage

Previewing Activities

- Teachers of all types of students may wish to have them read about the culture of the Amish prior to watching this movie. Suggested readings include "The Plain People of Pennsylvania," *in National Geographic.*

- Teachers might lead a discussion on the subject of guns and their role in law enforcement and crime prevention.

- Teachers of ESL students might wish to lead a discussion about the distinguishing characteristics of traditional religious minorities in the students' home countries.

Viewing Activities

GOOD PLACES TO STOP TO TALK

- In the most critical scene in this movie, Book, having been wounded in a shoot out in an underground garage, realizes that his boss is the person who has set him up. Teachers may wish to stop the film at this point to check for comprehension.

Bracknell and Wokingham College

- Teachers may wish to have students track Book's responses to violence and how they change in the course of the movie. Teachers may also wish to have students track the Amish response to guns and violence and discuss them at the end of the film.

Follow-Up Activities

- Teachers might lead a discussion centered on the many religious and legal meanings of the word *witness* and how those many meanings are dealt with in the course of this movie.

- Teachers may have students rewrite the ending of the movie, imagining what Book's life would have been like if he had stayed, or what Rachel's life would have been like if she had gone with him.

Activities for Low-Level ESL Student

The following activities are suggested for use with low-level ESL students. A teacher can:

- show the murder scene to half the class. Have the rest of the class interview those who saw the scene to find out what they "witnessed." Write up police reports.

- show the scene in which Samuel finds the picture of the killer in the police station. Then have the students write an "action" script, in which they detail the specific movements of each of the people in the police station during the scene.

- play the scene in which Book is wounded and do a cloze passage of the voice-over. Discuss the meaning of this scene so that all students understand that Book's boss is crooked.

- play the scene in which Samuel finds the gun in the drawer, the scene in which Samuel and his grandfather discuss the gun, and the scene in which the Amish man is confronted by a redneck who "paints" him with ice cream. Then ask the students to write a profile of the Amish attitude toward violence and guns.

- do a cloze passage of the song "Wonderful World" by Art Garfunkle, stressing the subject words *biology, history, geography*. Play the scene in which Book and Rachel dance to this song in the barn and ask the students why they think this song was used as the background music.

- play the telephone conversation between Book's boss and the Lancaster sheriff. Have half the class listen for the boss's part and the other half listen for the sheriff's part. Afterward, discuss how the sheriff feels about the boss and how the boss feels about the sheriff.

Other Considerations

None.

Ancillary Material

Lee, Doug. "The Plain People of Pennsylvania." *National Geographic,* April 1984: 492–519.

The Wizard of Oz

Subjects:	1, 3, 17, 18, 20, 22	**Director:**	Victor Fleming
Playing Time:	101 minutes	**Producer:**	Mervyn LeRoy
Rating:	not rated in the U.S.	**Date:**	1939
		Actors:	Judy Garland, Bert Lahr, Margaret Hamilton, Ray Bolger, Jack Haley, Billie Burke, Frank Morgan

Plot Summary

Dorothy and her dog Toto live on a farm in rural Kansas with her aunt and uncle. One day a twister sucks up Dorothy and Toto. When she awakens, she is in a fantasy land, Oz. There she meets little Munchkins and a good witch who gives her a pair of ruby slippers. She wants to get back home, but the only way to get there is to find the Wizard of Oz in the Emerald City. On her journey along the yellow brick road she meets the Scarecrow, the Tin Man, and the Cowardly Lion, who accompany her. The wizard assigns them the "impossible" task of killing the Wicked Witch of the West and then renegs on his promise to send them back to Kansas. Dorothy, however, finds that she has always had the power to return home. Finally, bidding her new friends good-bye, she clicks her heels three times and she's back in Kansas. Auntie Em and Uncle Henry never looked better.

General Commentary

This is a classic fantasy! Besides the great cinematography, the songs in this musical are unforgettable. Teachers can use the film when teaching the growth of Populism in America in the late 1890s, as well as metaphor. Since many Americans think the movie is as American as apple pie, it is an excellent choice for an ESL class.

Suggested Usage

Previewing Activities

- Teachers may have students read the book *Wizard of Oz* by L. Frank Baum.
- Teachers may want students to study the Populist movement of the late 1800s.
- Teachers can discuss metaphor.
- ESL teachers may want to preteach some of the movie's songs.

Viewing Activities

Good Places to Stop and Talk

- If students have read the book, teachers can stop the film after scenes that differ from the book and have students discuss how they are different.

- Teachers can also have students speculate about how this movie is a metaphor for Populism. The following questions may help students identify elements of the metaphor: What do the characters Dorothy meets represent? What does the yellow brick road represent?

Follow-up Activities

- The teacher may want to have the students read Peter Dreier's article "*The Wizard of Oz*: A Political Fable" to find out what the different elements in the movie really mean with regard to Populism.

- Teachers may want to review the book, the movie, and the article by Littlefield and have students write an analysis of some of the characters and people or ideas Littlefield thinks they represent.

- Teachers may show *The Wiz*, a 1978 African-American remake of the movie, and then have the students compare the two movies orally.

- Students can write a comparison and contrast between the movie and the novel.

Other Considerations

This is a must-see movie.

Ancillary Material

Baum, Frank L. *The Wizard of Oz*. New York: Macmillan, 1962.

Dreier, Peter. "*The Wizard of Oz*: A Political Fable." *Today Journal*. Feb. 14, 1986.

Langley, Noel, Florence Ryerson, and Edgar Allan Wolf. *The Wizard of Oz: The Screenplay*. New York: Delta, 1989.

The Wiz. Directed by Sidney Lumet. Universal/Motown, 1978.

A World Apart

Subjects:	7, 13, 14, 14, 22, 23	**Director:**	Chris Menges
Playing Time:	112 minutes	**Producer:**	Sara Radclyffe
Rating:	PG	**Date:**	1988
		Actors:	Barbara Hershey, Jodhi May, Jeroen Krabbe

Plot Summary

This biographical film is set in Johannesburg, South Africa, in 1963. Diana Roth is a journalist and single mother trying to raise three girls on her own, after her husband an ANC (African National Council) official, disappears. Molly Roth is the thirteen-year-old daughter whose life of privilege is disrupted by her mother's involvement in certain political activities. The film examines the relationship between a politically active white mother and her teen-age daughter in racially divided South Africa.

General Commentary

Although this film is considered a well-constructed indictment on apartheid, it explores the issue through the eyes of white South Africans. Two black African characters are developed in some depth: Elsie, the family's maid, and her brother Solomon, a political activist. Teachers can use this film with students studying apartheid, civil rights, or South Africa in general.

Suggested Usage

Previewing Activities

- The teacher could have the students define the word *apartheid*.
- The teacher may have the students research the history of apartheid in South Africa and create a time line of events from the beginning of apartheid up to 1963.

Viewing Activities

GOOD PLACES TO STOP AND TALK

- Molly's discovery of the truth of a friend's rejection can illustrate the pain that apartheid causes and is a good place to stop and ask the students to discuss Molly and her friend's dilemma.
- Another scene that may help students understand the political climate is the scene in which Diana wrongly thinks she is to be released from prison. This scene can be used to open a discussion on human rights and the "90-Day Detention Act."

- Numerous scenes focus on the pain and suffering of those hurt by the apartheid of South Africa. In addition to the scenes above, a funeral for a murdered black man manifests the hurt the family and community feel. Teachers may want to have their students record the different ways individuals and groups are affected and deal with the pain and suffering.

Follow-up Activities

- The teacher might have students complete the time line that they started in the previewing activities (from 1963 to the present).
- The teacher may assign students a reading from Nadine Gordimer.
- Students who are interested in the first-hand accounts of the time may want to read *117 Days* by Ruth First.
- Students can research and report on the state of racial affairs in the United States during the early 1960s.
- Students can research and report on what is happening in South Africa today.

Other Considerations

Secondary teachers should note that although the film was given a PG rating, some scenes could disturb some teenagers.

Ancillary Materials

First, Ruth. *117 Days*. New York: Stein & Day, 1965.

Gordimer, Nadine. *Selected Stories*. London: J. Cape, 1975.

Gordimer, Nadine. *Jump and Other Stories*. New York: Farrar, Strauss & Giroux, 1991.

Gordimer, Nadine, and David Goldblatt. *Lifetimes Under Apartheid*. New York: Alfred A. Knopf, 1986.

The Year of Living Dangerously

Subjects: 1, 14, 22, 23, 25
Playing Time: 115 minutes
Rating: PG

Director: Peter Weir
Producer: James McElroy
Date: 1983
Actors: Mel Gibson, Sigourney Weaver, Linda Hunt

Plot Summary

An Australian journalist, Guy Hamilton, and a British Embassy employee, Jill Bryant, are in Indonesia in the days prior to an attempted Communist coup against the Sukarno regime in the middle 1960s. Woven into the story of their romance is his development as a journalist. Tipped off by Jill that a Communist coup is about to happen, Hamilton is torn between loyalty and the desire to further his journalistic career. Should he follow the tip and expose Jill as his source, or should he accept the tip as it was intended: as a warning to leave Indonesia? Also blended into the story is Billy Kwan, a mysterious man who introduces Jill and Hamilton, and who seems to be cast in the role of conscience of the movie. It is Billy who introduces Hamilton to the dark side of Indonesia, and Billy who eventually martyrs himself to protest the treatment of the poor at the hands of Sukarno.

General Commentary

This is a lush period piece. The total experience of the movie is better than any one character or scene, with the possible exception of Billy Kwan, who is played by the female actress Linda Hunt. This movie offers some history, some geography, some political commentary, and a bit of moral dilemma. Any of these can be exploited with a secondary, post-secondary or intermediate / advanced ESL class.

Suggested Usage

Previewing Activities

- It is difficult to understand this movie without some background in the political climate in Indonesia in the 1960s. Teachers could have students research in encyclopedias and newspapers such topics as Sukarno and Indonesia in the 1960s.

- Teachers may want students to focus their research on the reasons for the popularity of Communism as a political system in Asian countries. Students could be challenged to explore why Communism caught on, or was at least attempted, in such countries as China, Cambodia, Vietnam, and North Korea. As they watch the movie, students could look for those features of Indonesian life in the 1960s that might have predisposed people to consider Communism as a viable political system.

Viewing Activities

Good Places to Stop and Talk

- A few major moral questions are raised in this movie, and in a few places students should be asked to think about what a character should / might do, including the scene in which Jill tells Hamilton that there will be a Communist coup and offers him help in getting out of Indonesia. Students could consider whether he should use this information for journalistic purposes or whether he should take Jill up on her offer. Another good scene is the scene in which Hamilton, with both eyes bound, is visited by his driver. Before his driver, who is a Communist, reports that the coup has failed, teachers can have students predict what the nature of his visit will be.

Patterns/Structures to Look For

- The character of Billy Kwan, like Jiminy Cricket in *Pinnochio*, is the voice of conscience in the movie. Students can watch for scenes in which Billy raises a moral question. They can discuss these scenes using these basic questions:

    What question is being raised?

    Why is Billy raising it?

    How is the question received?

    What will Billy do?

    What will the others do?

Follow-up Activities

- Several topics can / should be addressed in post-viewing discussions: the image of white people in the film, the image of journalists in the film, the image of Sukarno in this film, and the image of Communists in the film. Students should support any comments they make with specific examples from the film.

- Students can do research on the subsequent history of Indonesia, and Sukarno in particular, and do either oral or written reports. Students can focus their research on how conditions in Indonesia have changed, if at all, since the time of this film.

Other Considerations

There is one post-coital bedroom scene and some discussion of and allusion to lewd behavior.

TITLE INDEX

SUBJECT INDEX

1. ADVENTURE

2. AFRICAN-AMERICANS

3. AMERICAN HISTORY

4. AMERICAN SOCIETY (problems and aspects of)

5. ANIMATION

6. ASIANS

7. BIOGRAPHY

8. COLD WAR

9. COMEDY

10. COMING OF AGE

14. HISTORY, WORLD

17. LITERATURE AND/OR POETRY (Movies with accompanying reading.)

18. METAPHOR

19. MILITARY

23. RACE RELATIONS (International and Domestic)

24. RELIGION (Catholics, Protestants, Jews, Moslems, Hindus)

25. ROMANCE

29. WESTERNS

30. WORLD WAR I

31. LOW-LEVEL ESL MOVIES